Agenda **heroin**

THIS IS A CARLTON BOOK

Design copyright © 2000 Carlton Books Limited
Text copyright © 2000 Carlton Books Limited
Pictures © various, see Picture Acknowledgements

This edition published by Carlton Books Limited 2000
20 Mortimer Street
London
W1N 7RD

A CIP catalogue for this book is available from the British Library.

ISBN 1 85868 921 X

Design: Adam Wright/bluefrog
Picture research: Alex Pepper
Production: Garry Lewis

Agenda

heroin

Julian Durlacher

CARLTON
BOOKS

CONTENTS

PICTURE ACKNOWLEDGEMENTS

The publishers would like to thank the following sources for their kind permission to reproduce the pictures in this book:

Corbis/AFP 6, 69/Bettmann 9, 13, 28, 30, 40/Ric Ergenbright 75 /Everett 25, 50/Catherine Karnow 65/Christophe Loviny 77/Sean Sexton Collection 72/Underwood & Underwood 58

et archive 81, 93

Hulton Getty 18-19, 34, 36

Every effort has been made to acknowledge correctly and contact the source and/or copyright holder of each picture. Carlton Books Limited apologises for any unintentional errors or omissions, which will be corrected in future editions of this book.

INTRODUCTION

Illicit drugs are one of the biggest leisure activities in the world today, representing an estimated US$400 billion per annum industry. During the twentieth century they moved, despite the best efforts of governments and law enforcers, from the underground into the mainstream. This series of books tells the stories of these drugs, from their initial synthesis and use as therapeutic or medical aids, to their adoption as adjutants to pleasure. It also tells of the increasingly draconian legislation attendant as each drug moved from the medical to the sybaritic world.

Heroin was first synthesized in 1874 and was promoted some 25 years later as a cough remedy. Within years it had become a symbol of degradation and transgression, an image it has never lost. Yet production increases, despite all efforts to prevent its manufacture and use. Heroin explains why that is, from the misguided attempts at legislation at the beginning of the twentieth century to the entrenched attitudes of governments throughout it.

EARLY YEARS

THE WONDER DRUG

Not every cough medicine is featured in books, films, newspapers, government legislation and guerrilla warfare, but then heroin never was just any old cough medicine. Right from the start it was going to be something special, something "heroic".

Heroin was first produced in 1874 by C. R. Alder Wright, a chemist at St Mary's Hospital in London (where Alexander Fleming discovered Penicillin half a century later). He was experimenting with the opium derivative morphine (itself discovered in 1806) in an attempt to find the "essence" of opium. This was something of a Holy Grail in medicine at the time: opium and morphine were the only effective painkillers of the day, but there was growing concern over their addictive nature. It was thought that if you filtered out the "addictive" properties of opium you would be left with only the therapeutic essence. Wright passed some of this new substance on to a colleague, who tested it on animals. He found that it produced:

"Great prostration, fear, sleepiness speedily following administration, the eyes being sensitive and pupils dilated, considerable salivation being produced in dogs, and slight tendency to vomiting in some cases...Respiration was at first quickened but subsequently reduced, and the heart's action was diminished and rendered irregular. Marked want of co-ordinating power over the muscular movements and the loss of power in the pelvis and hind limbs...were the most noticeable effects."

Not surprisingly, Wright shelved his new discovery. Others also experimented with heroin over the next few years but none saw a future for it, except for Heinrich Dreser. Dreser was in charge of testing new drugs at Bayer, the German dye maker turned pharmaceutical company. He was a man of considerable flair and

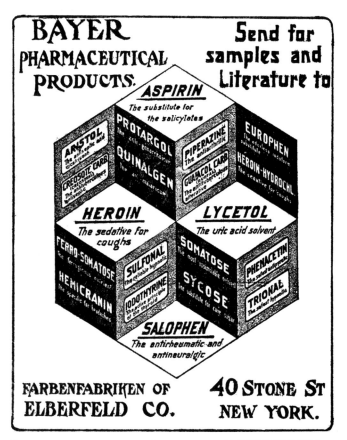

formidable personality. He also had a habit of taking the credit for his assistants' work and claiming the rewards – he earned a percentage of the profits from any new drug that was tested at his instigation. In 1897, one of his assistants, Felix Hoffman, presented him with two new compounds: acetylsalicylic acid and diacetylmorphine. The first of these is now better known as aspirin, the second as heroin. Dreser tested them both and decided there was no future for aspirin (*"That is typical... hot air,"* he said of encouraging reports. *"The product is worthless!"*) and nailed his colours to heroin. Having tested it on animals and then humans (including himself) he pronounced it effective in the treatment of a variety of respiratory ailments. These ailments included the bugbears of the nineteenth century – tuberculosis, bronchitis and asthma – as well as other disorders that were both incapacitating and incurable. Heroin seemed to help and, better still, according to Dreser, was not addictive. There was even talk of using heroin to wean people off morphine – it would be the methadone of its day. Bayer registered the new drug as "heroin", from the German word "heroisch", meaning "heroic".

Heroin looked like a gold-mine for both Dreser and Bayer. The company embarked on a massive marketing campaign, commending their new drug to doctors with free samples and the nineteenth-century equivalent of logo-marked diaries and ball-point pens. The response was phenomenal, with Bayer exporting heroin to twenty-three countries within the year. In the USA, the Saint James Society mounted a campaign to supply free samples of heroin to morphine addicts who were trying to give up the habit. Meanwhile, at Dreser's insistence, acetylsalicylic acid was put on the back-burner.

Soon, alarm bells began to ring. By the early 1900s, doctors and pharmacists noticed their patients were consuming an immoderate quantity of cough remedies laced with heroin. In 1911, the British Pharmaceutical Codex noted that heroin was as addictive as morphine and, in 1913, Bayer ceased production altogether. Happily for them, Hoffman had covertly been testing aspirin and was able to present findings confirming its efficacy. Dreser, previously so dismissive, belatedly recognized its virtues and with his usual cheek claimed the drug as his own. In a neat change of roles, heroin was now edged out of the scene and aspirin promoted as the new wonder drug. Dreser and Bayer, who do not mention heroin in their official history, made their fortune after all from the previously spurned aspirin. A lot of others made a fortune out of heroin as it swiftly superseded opium and morphine as the major drug of addiction.

Heroin's popularity rests on a variety of factors: firstly it is addictive, secondly it is illegal and thirdly there is big money in it. The first of these is no one's fault but the drug's – heroin just is physiologically addictive. The second two – heroin's illegality and the consequent profits involved in its trade – need explaining.

TEMPERANCE AND THE "YELLOW PERIL"

For some time in the West, an anti-opium movement had been simmering away, fuelled both by medical concerns and a growing Christian temperance movement. In 1900, Dr John Witherspoon, later President of the American Medical Association (AMA), delivered a speech to the Association warning of the medical community's duty to *"save our people from the clutches of this hydra-headed monster which stalks abroad through the civilized world, wrecking lives and happy homes, filling our jails and lunatic asylums, and taking from these unfortunates, the precious promises of eternal life."*

The statement is interesting because it combines the various features that were to characterize the discussion of opium and heroin throughout the century – a strange mixture of genuine medical concern and apocalyptic, moralistic bombast.

Things had come to a head in 1898 when the USA acquired the Philippines in the Spanish War. Charles Henry Brent was sent out as the first Protestant bishop of America's new colony. An ardent missionary, he wrote that he came to the Philippines in order *"to serve the nation and the kingdom of righteousness."* To this end, he set about converting the non-Christians of his diocese: be they *"pagan Igorots of the mountains of Luzon, the Muslims of the southern islands,* [or] *the Chinese settlements in Manila."* But more than mere paganism was afoot in the Philippines. He reported back home that opium addiction was rife, not just among the Chinese settlers but also – thanks to them – among the natives and – horror of horrors – US soldiers stationed there. A report on the situation was quickly commissioned and one of its findings alarmed the US government:

"While it has not been practicable to obtain exact figures, it can be stated that the drug habit is alarmingly increasing among the men of our army and navy. The number of men using opium in the army has greatly increased since the occupation of the Philippines, many 'opium smokers' acquiring the habit there from Chinese or natives. To the best of the writer's knowledge – and he has carefully inquired into facts – practically all the cases of drug habitués in both army and navy arise from the men learning the habit from natives of foreign countries or from lewd women and men in this country [the Philippines]*."*

In response, the US Government outlawed the importation of opium in any form except by the USA, and banned all non-medicinal uses. This was but the first in many national and international measures intended to combat the use of opium and, like them, it had an altogether unwelcome knock-on effect – the growth of an illegal market. Opium was smuggled in from China and heroin – until now unheard of outside the West – from Europe.

The US Government, flushed with its "success" in the Philippines, decided to expand its anti-drugs crusade. The USA was by now the wealthiest and most powerful country in the world, but one lacking the voice of authority still held by the old European powers, especially the UK. Opium was a cause in which the US had a head start and which they could use to demonstrate their status as a superpower. Best of all, they could take a swipe at the British, their rivals, while making friends with the Chinese, an important trading partner.

BRITAIN'S OPIUM TRADE

For years, Europeans, primarily the British, had been making a lot of money out of Chinese opium addicts. Having created a massive population of addicts in China – estimated at 27 per cent of the adult male population in 1900 – they supplied the opium from India to sustain them. China was not always amenable to this practice. In 1839, Emperor Tao Kwang sent a personal emissary, Commissioner Lin Tse-hsu, to Canton to tackle the situation. Lin first appealed directly for help to Queen Victoria, who had acceded to the British throne two years earlier at the age of eighteen:

"We have heard that in your Honourable Barbarian Country the people are not permitted to inhale the drug," wrote Commissioner Tse-hsu. *"If it is admittedly so deleterious, how can your seeking profit by exposing others to its malefic power be reconciled with the decrees of heaven? You should immediately have the plant plucked up by the very root. Cause the land there to be hoed up afresh, sow the five grains and if any man dare again to plant a single poppy, visit his crime with condign punishment. Then not only will the people of this Celestial Kingdom be delivered from an intolerable evil, but your own barbarian subjects, albeit forbidden to indulge, will be safeguarded against falling a prey to temptation. There will result for each the enjoyment of felicity.*

"We have reflected, that this noxious article is the clandestine manufacture of artful schemers under the dominion of your honourable nation. Doubtless, you, the Honourable Chieftainess, have not commanded the growing and sale thereof."

Victoria did not deign to reply and any attempts to interrupt the flow of opium to China were met with punitive measures – the British fought two wars over this issue in the nineteenth century. Toward the end of the century, groups such as the Anglo-Oriental Society for the Suppression of the Opium Trade, which numbered among its supporters the Archbishop of Canterbury, began to voice concern and questions were raised in the houses of parliament about a practice *"utterly inconsistent with the honour and duty of a Christian kingdom."* In 1907, under pressure from home and the USA, the UK finally ended the opium trade with China, leaving the country's millions of addicts to fend for themselves. Inevitably, as in the Philippines, Chinese addicts did not simply give up. Since the nineteenth century, China had been growing its own opium in an attempt to free itself of its dependence on imports. They never reached self sufficiency while Britain and others were still supplying the goods, but after 1907, assisted by a politically chaotic situation, they went into overdrive. Before long, they would be producing a surplus and, in what must have felt like poetic justice, sending it back to the people who had got them hooked in the first place.

The USA, again eager to seize the initiative, called for an international conference on the opium problem. This was becoming a matter of some urgency as opium was increasingly being seen as not just a foreign problem, but a domestic one too. Throughout the nineteenth century, opiate addiction was rife in America. Remedies containing morphine and opium were freely available without prescription and little stigma was attached to their use. Patent medicines were packed with them, be they cures for morning sickness or colic. The majority of addicts were respectable middle-class women who had become dependent on the drug through repeated prescriptions.

Opium smoking had at one time been largely restricted to the

"ONE OF THE MOST FERTILE CAUSES OF UNHAPPINESS IN THE UNITED STATES" - THE OPIUM DEN

immigrant Chinese community, but during the latter half of the century white Americans began to take up the habit. Figures such as Dr Hamilton Wright, the newly appointed United States opium commissioner, were quick to appreciate the problem: *"The* [opium] *habit,"* he said in an interview to the *New York Times,* *"has this Nation in its grip to an astonishing extent. Our prisons and our hospitals are full of victims of it, it has robbed ten thousand business men of moral sense and made them beasts who prey upon their fellows, unidentified it has become one of the most fertile causes of unhappiness and sin in the United States, if not the cause which can be charged with more of both than any other."* But where were people acquiring this habit? Wright again: *"One of the most unfortunate phases of the habit of smoking opium in this country* [was] *the large number of women who have become involved and were living as common-law wives or cohabiting with Chinese in the Chinatowns of our various cities."*

Early on in the campaign against opium emerged a theme that proved far more powerful than the idea of temperance – racism. Opium was labelled as a Chinese vice, contaminating the nation's youth. Sensationalist stories in the press about Chinese laundries and their links with white slave traders abounded. The first Fu-Manchu story was written at this time, where the evil mastermind is described as:

"...tall, lean and feline, high-shouldered, with a brow like Shakespeare and a face like Satan, a close-shaven skull, and long, magnetic eyes of the true cat-green...with all the cruel cunning of an entire Eastern race, accumulated in one giant intellect, with all the resources of science past and present, with all the resources, if you will, of a wealthy government – which, however, already has denied all knowledge of his existence. Imagine that awful being, and you have a mental picture of Dr Fu-Manchu, the yellow peril incarnate in one man."

It would have been of little use to point out that opium, far from being a "Chinese vice," had been cultivated in China by European colonists for their own profit. Nor that successive Chinese Emperors had tried to resist this debilitation of their population, periodically banning the use and production of opium long before the West had ever thought about prohibition. The race issue "had legs" then just as it does now and was played to the full by characters such as Wright and Brent.

AMERICA LEADS THE WAY

A commission (it was downgraded from a conference, much to the United States' chagrin) was convened in Shanghai in 1909, chaired by the ubiquitous Bishop Brent. The USA sent as their representative Dr

Wright, who later pointed out America's credentials as the leader in what was becoming an international crusade:

"The conference [sic] *was held and stimulated interest throughout the nations of the earth. We had become leaders in a real world movement looking to a great reform and had just reason to be proud of this; but we had gone to Shanghai fresh from our achievements in the* [Philippine] *islands with a great feeling that we were a righteous crowd licensed to feel superior...This situation on the islands, with the study it gave rise to, led us toward some appreciation of our own domestic faults and earnest efforts to correct them, so, after all, even the worst enemies of the Pacific islands must acknowledge that they have been beneficial in their general effect on us. Without the work which their necessities demanded it is doubtful if we would today be so near to general appreciation of the hold which drugs have taken on us as a nation. Our action in the islands, too, was destined to prove beneficial, not to us, alone, but to the world at large, for the traffic in the islands was not only very rapidly suppressed, but the attention of the great community of nations was attracted by our discoveries and action, to the problem and, later, to the possibilities of its solution."*

The Shanghai commission came up with a set of recommendations limiting the use and importation of opium. As they were only recommendations they were unenforceable under international law (itself a novelty), but Shanghai was the first step in a long history of increasingly restrictive measures both international and national.

In 1914, the Harrison Act was passed by the US congress. This act stipulated that *"all persons who produce, import, manufacture, compound, deal in, dispense, sell, distribute, or give away opium or coca leaves, their salts, derivatives, or preparations"* be licensed and liable to a tax. It went on to say that *"Nothing contained in this section shall apply...to the dispensing or distribution of any of the aforesaid drugs to a patient by a physician, dentist, or veterinary surgeon registered under this Act in the course of his professional practice only."*

It was this last, seemingly innocuous, phrase that law enforcement officers and the courts seized upon. "Professional practice only" was understood as excluding the maintenance of addiction, which was not seen as a disease. Thus any physician prescribing opiates to an addict would be subject to imprisonment. The Harrison Act, framed largely by Hamilton Wright, effectively enshrined the idea of addict as criminal, an idea that has dominated and frustrated drug debate ever since.

Just one year after the Harrison Act was passed, an editorial in *American Medicine* reported:

"Narcotic drug addiction is one of the gravest and most important questions confronting the medical profession today. Instead of improving conditions, the laws recently passed have made the problem more complex. Honest medical men have found such handicaps and dangers to themselves and their reputations in these laws...that they have simply decided to have as little to do as possible with drug addicts or their needs...The druggists are in the same position and for similar reasons many of them have discontinued entirely the sale of narcotic drugs. [The addict] *is denied the medical care he urgently needs, open, above-board sources from which he formerly obtained his drug supply are closed to him, and he is driven to the underworld where he can get his drug, but of course, surreptitiously and in violation of the law...*

"Abuses in the sale of narcotic drugs are increasing... A particular sinister sequence... is the character of the places to which [addicts] *are forced to go to get their drugs and the type of people with whom they are obliged to mix. The most depraved criminals are often the dispensers of these habit-forming drugs. The moral dangers, as well as the effect on the self-respect of the addict, call for no comment. One has only to think of the stress under which the addict lives, and to recall his lack of funds, to realize the extent to which these... afflicted individuals are under the control of the worst elements of society.*

"In respect to female habituées the conditions are worse, if possible. Houses of ill fame are usually their sources of supply, and one has only to think of what repeated visitations to such places mean to countless good women and girls – unblemished in most instances except for an unfortunate addiction to some narcotic drug – to appreciate the terrible menace."

The Harrison Act, far from eliminating opiate use, had just rendered it criminal. A report of the Special Committee of the Treasury Department, in 1918, stated that: *"In recent years, especially since the enactment of the Harrison law, the traffic by 'underground' channels has increased enormously, and at the present time it is believed to be equally as extensive as that carried on in a legitimate manner!"*

While legal access to heroin was now more difficult, there was no shortage of the drug. Bayer had never patented the heroin production process – it was not, after all, their discovery – so anyone could make it and plenty did: there were still over 120 factories legally producing heroin in 1920. Consequently, after the Harrison Act more heroin was being produced than there was a legal, medical need for. But for the enterprising manufacturer, this did not create a problem, but rather an opportunity. Surplus heroin was siphoned off to the black market, where it proved a prodigious success.

Heroin was the perfect illicit drug: it is easily adulterated, meaning greater profit margins for dealers. Its relative compactness means it can easily be hidden about the person; being more concentrated than either morphine or opium, you need a smaller quantity to achieve the same effect. Heroin was also cheaper than either morphine or opium and had the added attraction that it could be sniffed rather than injected. From the dealer's point of view, it also offered the great bonus of being addictive. Hence heroin manufactured in Europe found its way on to the streets of the USA and China and by the 1930s heroin had almost completely supplanted morphine as the narcotic drug of choice in these two countries.

JUNKIES

While the first American addicts may well have been introduced to the drug by their doctors, these were soon a minority. *"The present heroin habitué,"* wrote a doctor in *the New Republic* in 1913, *"rarely accuses a physician of being the one who introduced him to his cruel master. The first dose of heroin is neither pill nor hypodermic injection taken to alleviate some physical distress, but is a minute quantity of a fine powder 'blown' up the nose at the suggestion of an agreeable companion who has tried it and found it 'fine'."*

Clearly, this is not a description of a housewife with a cough or a child with bronchitis – the supposed recipients of heroin. The majority of heroin users in the USA at the beginning of the twentieth century were young, white, working-class men who took the drug for purely "recreational" reasons. Often they were gang members and taking heroin was part of the initiation process. It was in this era that the term "junky" first appeared – coined to describe addicts who stole junk metal to support their habit. The use of drugs for recreational purposes was nothing new, opium smoking had been growing throughout the West and was almost endemic in China at the time, but the almost immediate association of heroin with criminality was. This association was to grow once those other bogeymen of the twentieth century – the Mafia – got involved.

THE CZAR OF CRIME

In the early days, the illicit heroin business was run mainly by the Jewish gangs. Slang terms of Yiddish origin such as "schmecher" (an addict) and "smack" (heroin) testify to this connection. The Italians disapproved of both drugs and prostitution, preferring to stick to more "honourable" activities like the "numbers game" (gambling), the black market and, from 1920, bootlegging (illicit alcohol production). But Salvatore Lucania, aka Charles "Lucky" Luciano, changed all

"LUCKY" LUCIANO AND FRIENDS, IN HIS NATIVE SICILY, FROM WHERE HE
MASTERMINDED HIS INTERNATIONAL DRUG SMUGGLING OPERATIONS

that. Born in Sicily, in 1897, he moved to New York in 1907 with his
family and, precocious from the start, was arrested the same year for
shoplifting. In his teens, he worked as a delivery boy for a hat maker,
but supplemented his earnings by delivering heroin for a local pusher.
He would hide the drugs in the hat bands of deliveries he was making
– an early example of the ingenuity that heroin smugglers were to
demonstrate over the years and a testament to the ease with which
heroin can be concealed. But this was just the beginning of a criminal
career that would later earn him the title of "the Czar of organized

crime," and, according to *Time* magazine, one of twenty "builders and titans" of the twentieth century, along with Henry Ford, Bill Gates and Walt Disney.

Luciano's rise to power was effected by the traditional method of having his bosses assassinated. Once there, however, his methods were less strong-arm Mafia and more boardroom corporate. In 1931, with his childhood friend, Meyer Lansky (the head of Murder Inc., which hired out contract killers) he brought together the various gang families and nationalities and created the Commission, which ran in much the same way as any other major business. It had a board of directors and, perhaps mindful of Al Capone's downfall at the hands of the Internal Revenue Service (IRS), even paid (some) taxes. *"I'll bet in those days,"* he once said, *"we had a bigger company than Henry Ford.... We had exporters and importers, all kinds of help that any corporation needs, only we had more. And we had lawyers by the carload, and they was on call twenty-four hours a day."*

Luciano had no time for the "old ways." He saw there was money to be made in prostitution and soon became one of the biggest pimps in town. But foreseeing the end of alcohol prohibition, he cornered the illegal drug market. Luciano dragged the Mafia into the modern age and it is largely due to him that the link between the Mafia and drug trafficking was established.

The association with heroin of that peculiarly twentieth-century bogeyman, organized crime, was to provide yet more fruitful ground for the proselytizers and legislators of the day. Two figures stood at the forefront of the crusade and did as much as any to maintain the level of public hysteria necessary for the enactment of increasingly draconian legislation. One was Richmond Pearson Hobson, the other Henry J. Anslinger.

MOVERS AND SHAKERS

Hobson was a hero of the Spanish War – officially anyway. In 1898, in a botched attempt to block the Spanish Fleet in Santiago harbour, Cuba, he sank his own ship, was captured and spent most of the war in a Spanish prison in Cuba. On his return to America after the war, the Navy decorated him rather than face the ignominy of telling the world about his hair-brained scheme and Hobson became the *"most kissed man in America."* In 1906 he was elected to congress. Benson viewed himself as an example of *"Homeric manhood, erect and masterful,"* and needed a suitably heroic cause to attach himself to. He started with the imminent (and imagined) threat of a Japanese invasion.

Despite his heroic status press, public and president soon tired of his rantings and he looked elsewhere for a cause. He found it in prohibition. Hobson had always been a man of high moral principles. At the naval academy, he had been shunned by his contemporaries because of his strong religious views and his tendency to sneak on class-mates. In a series of lectures, he detailed the dangers of alcohol:

"Alcohol is killing our people at the rate of nearly two thousand men a day, every day of the year," he said, adding *"one out of five children of alcohol consumers are hopelessly insane"* and *"ninety-five percent of all acts and crimes of violence are committed by drunkards."*

Quite where he got his statistics from remains a mystery to this day. In 1911, he proposed the first national prohibition act, but to no avail, and in 1916 he left congress. He continued rallying people to the cause of temperance until the US Government took the wind out of his sails by passing the Volstead act in 1917 and instigating prohibition. So he cast round for a new cause worthy of his concern. He found it in heroin, which had the distinction of combining both his previous crusades – against the East and against intemperance. *"Like the invasions and plagues of history, the scourge of narcotic drug addiction came out of Asia."* Substituting "heroin" for "alcohol" he produced yet more outrageous statistics. He mobilized the now underemployed Women's Christian Temperance Union and others and created the World Narcotic Association. In 1928, never one to mince his words, he claimed that:

"Most of the daylight robberies, daring hold-ups, cruel murders, and similar crimes of violence are now known to be committed chiefly by drug addicts who constitute the primary cause of our alarming crime wave... Drug addiction is more communicable and less curable than leprosy. Drug addicts are the principal carriers of vile disease, and with their lowered resistance are incubators and carriers of the streptococcus, pneumococcus, *the germ of flu, of tuberculosis and other diseases. New forces of narcotic drug exploitation devised from the progress of modern chemical science, added to the old form of the opium traffic, now endanger the very future of the human race... The whole human race, though largely ignorant on this subject, is now in the midst of a life and death struggle with the deadliest foe that has ever menaced its future. Upon the issue hangs the perpetuation of civilization, the destiny of the world and the future of the human race."*

Hobson adamantly subscribed to the idea of opiate addiction as contagious, an idea first propagated by Hamilton Wright, who said: *"A drinking man as a rule likes company in drinking, but will advise others, especially the young, to avoid his fate and go the other way. A heroin addict has literally a mania to lead others into addiction and will make every effort to do so, having no pity even for children."* He also stressed a recurrent theme in the century's drug rhetoric – the corruption of the young: *"The dope peddlers employ boys and girls to make addicts of their companions. Bearing in mind the psychology of the heroin addict, when a boy or girl becomes a heroin addict he starts almost immediately as a recruiting agent for the peddler."*

While Hobson was busy whipping up the good ladies of the USA into a frenzy of fear for their children, Anslinger was devoting himself to the *realpolitik* of getting ever greater controls against drug use and trafficking on to the statute books and, consequently, greater powers for his embryonic Federal Bureau of Narcotics (FBN). The FBN was a very junior partner as far as law enforcement went. The Federal Bureau of Investigation (FBI), headed by the all powerful J. Edgar Hoover, got all the press, all the praise and all the money. Anslinger was determined to build up his own dime store operation to rival Hoover's, with whom he had an immense and personal rivalry. To do so, he needed to build up the drug menace to the point where the USA needed him and his men to save them. Anslinger came to narcotics from an undistinguished career in the diplomatic corps, via a short spell in prohibition maintenance.

Anslinger was, according to one colleague, *"a grotesquely ugly man. Frightening... He had a disposition about him that used to scare the shit out of people..."* He hated communists, the Mafia and Drug dealers equally, at times to the point of paranoia. *"I believe especially,"* he wrote in his 1961 autobiography *The Murderers*, *"that we must be on guard against the use of drugs as a political weapon by the Communist forces in China and elsewhere in the orient, Europe and Africa. There is every chance that some of the commies and fellow travellers may join hands with the world-wide syndicate."* Happily for Anslinger, most of the American people at the time shared his prejudices.

More than any other individual, he is responsible for the way drugs are viewed and legislated against, not only in the USA but elsewhere in the world. He was dismissive of even the slightest hint of liberalism when it came to drugs, and denounced the idea of maintenance as merely pandering to the dealers. *"Much of the campaign for relaxing narcotic controls and setting up clinics emanates, in fact, from organized syndicate sources,"* he once claimed.

For years, Anslinger "massaged" statistics, at times making out that the drug problem was greater than it was, in order to justify the continued existence of his department, at other times, claiming huge reductions in the number of addicts, again in order to justify his department's existence. And so he was able to run the FBN (later the Drug Enforcement Agency) with an iron hand from its inception in 1930 until 1961, when he retired.

As the US domestic drug control movement gathered momentum, it became apparent that, in order to curtail drug use at home, supplies had to be cut off. Thus they further lobbied for international legislation and co-operation. They got it in 1925, when the League of Nations convened the Geneva Conference, launching a new round of drug diplomacy. Voluntary national laws were replaced by mandatory international controls. An 82 per cent decline in world (legal) opium supply ensued – from 42,000 tons in 1906 to 16,000 tons in 1934.

This decline was not, however, matched by a decline in the numbers of people wanting the drug. So, as soon as governments slashed imports or closed opium dens, smugglers and dealers emerged to service the unmet demand. Thailand and Indo-China found it impossible to close their mountain borders to the overland caravan trade from Yunnan and Burma (now Myanmar), the major producers of opium in the area. With 50 per cent of the region's smokers and 70 per cent of its dens, Bangkok and Saigon were South-east Asia's biggest opium markets, offering high profits which drew the caravans southward from the opium hills. Meanwhile, China's illicit opium production had mushroomed and with it a nascent heroin industry. Europeans had gone to Shanghai and used their expertise to set up illegal factories as conditions became more and more controlled back home. But by the 1930s the Chinese were running the business themselves, producing enough heroin not only for themselves but with enough on top to export.

LOST OPPORTUNITIES

The immediate post-war period should have been a high point in the lives of anti-drug campaigners. The Second World War severely limited the activities of the traffickers; with restrictions on shipping and tight port security, supplies to the USA from Europe and Asia went into free fall. Mexico tried to fill the breach but its product, "Mexican mud", was of inferior quality and insufficient quantity. Many US addicts were forced to quit or turn to painkillers or drink. By the end of the war, there were only 20,000 US addicts, an all-time low in the country. In China, the communist victory had almost overnight resulted in the eradication of their opium problem, admittedly by means that Anslinger, bound by the constraints of democracy, could only dream of. Anslinger, Benson et al had reason to be optimistic for the future of their mutual crusade, but things were to prove otherwise. The post-war period ushered in a new era in the history of the heroin trade, with new markets and new producers. What had gone before was just a taster.

LUCIANO EARNS HIS NICKNAME

Lucky Luciano's reign as the crime king of New York had not lasted long. In June 1936, he was sentenced to thirty to fifty years in prison for pimping. The authorities were well aware of his narcotic operations, but this was the only charge they could get to stick. Then, in 1946, he was suddenly released and deported back to Italy. Quite why is still shrouded in mystery but it does appear that the US military found it in their best interests to strike some sort of deal with him.

After the Japanese bombing of Pearl Harbor in 1941, military leaders became convinced that Nazi spies and saboteurs were operating in the New York docks, enabling the Germans to sink US merchant ships in coastal waters. The docks were one of Luciano's domains and, in desperation, US intelligence turned to him for help. Using his partner in crime, Meyer Lansky, as a go-between, they got Luciano to order the dock workers to report back to US intelligence. Now, they had an entire army of ears and eyes, thanks to Luciano.

The military had reason to turn to the Mafia again in 1943. They needed to be sure of a friendly reception in Sicily when they landed on the island to launch their invasion of Italy. Again, it is thought that Luciano, whose influence stretched across the Atlantic, helped to secure the co-operation of his compatriots. So, in 1946, a grateful and victorious nation released Luciano and deported him back to Italy.

It was not long before he was up to his old tricks again, this time based in Europe. It is one of the great "what ifs?" of history but, arguably, had the Japanese not bombed Pearl Harbor and Luciano, the king of American Narcotic trafficking, not been repatriated to Europe, that continent's future role in the drug business might have been very different. Luciano promptly set up illegal heroin laboratories in Sicily, processing morphine or opium from the Middle East. That he was able to do so with some ease is again a consequence of the Second World War.

THE FRENCH CONNECTION

After the war, the overriding concern of the West was the rising threat of Communism. In the exhausted and financially ruined states of Europe, the left was on the march. In Italy and France, the problem was seen as particularly severe, as many of the resistance, now heroes, were communists. The Mafia were equally ill-disposed toward communists and so a natural alliance was formed. The Central Intelligence Agency (CIA) funded the Mafia, who ensured that the communists lost the 1948 elections in Italy. Thus the Mafia regained their pre-war influence – with the support of grateful politicians they could do pretty much as they wished – and by 1950 once again controlled Sicily.

Luciano and his cohorts found themselves better off than ever, geographically located midway between the opium-producing regions and their main market and in a country where little attention was paid to their illegal activities. This golden period did not last long, however. In the 1950s, the Italian Government, under some pressure from the USA, started to crack down on the heroin laboratories in Sicily. This was, of course, only a minor inconvenience. Luciano and friends simply upped sticks and moved operations to Marseilles.

THE FRENCH CONNECTION WAS IMMORTALIZED IN THE OSCAR-WINNING FILM OF THE SAME NAME. HERE POPEYE DOYLE, PLAYED BY GENE HACKMAN, BRANDISHES THE EVIDENCE.

In post-war France, there prevailed a similar situation to that in Italy. The socialists had control of the docks and were refusing to load military supplies on ships bound for the French colony of Vietnam (formerly part of French Indo-China). Furthermore, France's political situation was as fragile as Italy's and the USA feared that the communists were taking over the trade unions. This time, the CIA and their French equivalent turned to the Corsicans. The Corsicans, who had long been running smuggling and prostitution operations in France, were the dominant criminal contingent in Marseilles. Assisted by funds from the CIA, they established control over the dockers' unions and the West was once again able to breathe easy – except that the Corsicans, having gained control of the docks, decided to use them for their own ends. The "French Connection" was born.

The French Connection, the smuggling of illicit heroin from Marseilles to North America, had been in existence before the war, but had always been subsidiary to Sicilian operations. Once these were shut down, however, Marseilles became the epicentre of European drug traffic. With control of the docks, the Corsicans could ensure that illegal shipments of opium or morphine could arrive safely. Furthermore, Marseilles was near a major perfume-producing area. One of the major ingredients used in the making of perfume is acetic anhydride. This is also one of the substances used in producing heroin. The Corsicans also had a tacit understanding with the French authorities. If they made sure that the heroin was for export only, and not for native consumption, the police were prepared to turn a blind eye.

It was estimated that, between 1951 and 1973, the French Connection accounted for 80 per cent of the United States' illegal heroin imports. The routes by which the drug was smuggled into America were many and often ingenious. One of the most favoured, as immortalized in the 1971 film *The French Connection*, was to hide the powder in secret compartments in a car and then ship the car over to the USA. But anything and everything was used to smuggle in heroin, from tins of Spanish "paella" to ski poles (in 1969 a New Jersey hairdresser was arrested in his attempt to import hundreds of them, each stuffed with 160 grams of heroin, into the USA).

THE GOLDEN TRIANGLE

Most of the raw product for heroin came from Turkey during the 1950s but then, in one of those periodic clampdowns that governments are prone to, in the 1960s the Turkish authorities decided to get tough and eradicate opium from their shores. The ever resourceful Corsicans merely went further afield, this time to South-east Asia – many Corsicans had settled in French Indo-China – and helped to create what has now become the biggest heroin and opium producer in the world, the "Golden Triangle". In South-east Asia, although opium use was widespread, opium production was limited, most of it intended for local use. In the absence of ready supplies from Turkey, production was stepped up. But it was more than a simple question of supply and demand. Once again, cold war politics entered the picture.

When Chiang Kai-shek's Nationalists (the Kuomintang, or KMT) were finally defeated by Mao Tse-tung's Communist army, many of them decamped to the Shan province of Burma. It is a rugged and inaccessible region on the border of China, tailor-made for a guerrilla army. It is also tailor-made for the growing of opium. The Chinese Nationalists quickly took over the opium trade there, using force if necessary to persuade local farmers to replace whatever they were growing with opium. Prices for opium were rocketing, reflecting an imbalance between supply and demand, thanks to international legislation and China's departure from the world drug scene. The KMT financed their ongoing and ultimately futile war against Communist China with the proceeds from opium. But the KMT were not the only ones who wanted to see an end to Mao's rule in China.

The USA was terrified at the prospect of another huge Communist power in the East. As the American Government saw it, the KMT –

capitalists to the core – were their best hope. The American Government sent in the CIA to help train and arm them for a series of invasions into Southern China. America could not itself attack China but it was prepared to assist (covertly) anyone else prepared to. It was thus in their interests to keep the KMT as strong and wealthy as possible and this meant, if not actively encouraging their opium activities, at the very least tolerating them. By the early 1960s, when this CIA operation finally ended, Burma's opium production had risen from fifteen to three hundred tons.

A similar situation prevailed in Laos, one of the other three countries (with Burma/Myanmar and Thailand) that comprise the "Golden Triangle", although this time the communist enemy was in Vietnam. When France was fighting Ho Chi-minh's Communist forces in Vietnam from 1950 to 1954, the military found themselves increasingly short of funds for covert operations. This they remedied by establishing control over the drug traffic that linked the Hmong poppy fields of Laos with the opium dens of Saigon, generating immense profits.

AIR TRAFFIC

When the USA gradually replaced the French in Vietnam after 1954, they inherited not only a colonial war but also a drug monopoly. The CIA used this as a source of funds to mount covert operations in both Vietnam and Laos. Their involvement with the drug trade went way beyond merely turning a blind eye. When the French left Laos in 1955, several hundred veterans from the war stayed on, among them a number of Corsicans. Many of these were trained pilots who set up small charter airlines, officially to ferry businessmen and diplomats around. But the small charter planes had a much more lucrative side-line – the transporting of opium to refineries in Thailand and Vietnam.

In 1965, the Corsican adventurers were put out of business by the simple expedient of having their rights to land at airports removed. Into their shoes stepped the CIA and their own airline, Air America. For the next five years, Air America, a small fleet of planes intended for the transport of CIA operatives and equipment, was used to convey large amounts of opium out of Laos.

After the war in Vietnam spilled over into Laos in 1965, the CIA recruited 30,000 Hmong highlanders into a secret army, making the tribe a vital CIA asset. Between 1965 and 1970, the Hmong guerrillas recovered downed US pilots, battled local communists, monitored the Ho Chi-minh Trail (the route through Laos by which North Vietnamese Communists infiltrated the South) and, most importantly, protected the radar that guided the US Air Force bombing of North Vietnam. The Hmong General, Vang Pao was a necessary ally for the CIA and

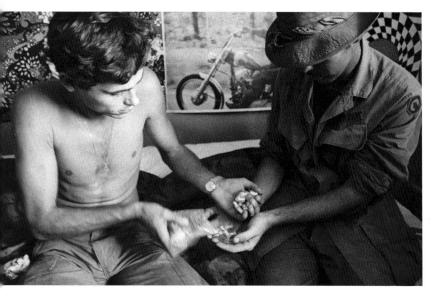

AMERICAN GIS PROVIDED A HUGE MARKET FOR THE "GOLDEN TRIANGLE" AND HELPED FOSTER A NASCENT HEROIN INDUSTRY

was therefore indulged at every turn. Before long, he was transformed from a minor tribal warlord into an all powerful drug lord. As long as the CIA needed him, they did little to interfere.

DOPED UP GIs

The Vietnam war was to have another far-reaching effect on the heroin trade. This time it was nothing to do with the CIA or covert actions, but the generation of a new market. By 1971 it was estimated that 10-15 per cent of American servicemen in Vietnam were hooked on heroin. In itself, this is not a significant statistic – research suggests that most GIs discontinued the habit upon their return. But it is important in that it instigated the first laboratories manufacturing high grade heroin in South-east Asia. Until that time, South-east Asia only had the capacity to produce lower grade, or brown, heroin – enough to satisfy the locals but not good enough for the American market. The good stuff was manufactured in Europe. But with a resident population of American soldiers it made sense to produce quality merchandise *in situ* rather than having to send opium to Europe and then import it back as heroin. By the end of the Vietnam War, not only had countless Americans and Vietnamese died but South-east Asia had been established as a major manufacturer of heroin, as well as a major producer of opium.

HEROIN AND CULTURE

THE COLOUR CARD

Before the Second World War, heroin was mainly seen as a working-class drug. For some, however, this has been part of its attraction – throughout the twentieth century, people have been drawn to heroin in rebellion or dissatisfaction. A notable exception to this was when a small group of smart Europeans – the "Happy Valley" set of English aristocrats in Kenya – discovered the drug in the 1930s. As will be explained later on, this was not to be the only connection between heroin and the English upper classes. Initially, recreational use of heroin was confined to young white men on the north-eastern seaboard of the USA. Their suppliers were, at first, corrupt pharmacists and then the Jewish and Italian gangs. This did not stop the polemicists of the day, such as Hamilton Wright and Hobson, blaming it on the Chinese. But soon they acquired new scapegoats, the black jazz musicians.

From 1910 to 1930, there was a huge migration of blacks from the southern states to the industrial north, looking for work. Quickly, they replaced the Chinese as the "problematic" immigrant population and lurid tales of "black rapists" began to replace stories of "Chinese white slave traders" in the press. Naturally, the blacks were claimed to have taken over the Chinese's other main supposed franchise – drugs. In their "campaign to corrupt America's youth" they were said to be assisted by their music.

The moral guardians of America were quick to draw the public's attention to the problem as they saw it: *"I can say from my own knowledge,"* went a report from the Illinois Vigilance Association in 1922, *"that about 50 per cent of our young boys and girls from the age of sixteen to twenty-five that land in the insane asylum these days are jazz-crazy dope fiends and public dance hall patrons. Jazz combinations – dope fiends and public dance halls – are the same. Where you find one you will find the other."*

Although this was all, of course, sheer nonsense, nonetheless drugs did play a huge part in the jazz scene. So strong was the link between jazz and drugs that the two share much of the same slang – "hip" started out as a term for an opium addict, referring to the callous he developed on his hip from resting his pipe there. "Cool", "crazy" and "jive" are all words that are shared between jazz and drugs. But this

SHOOTING UP IN THE EARLY YEARS OF THE TWENTIETH CENTURY - AN EYE DROP AND A SAFETY PIN AND A HELPING HAND ARE ALL YOU NEED

was not part of some grandiose plan to corrupt American youth, it was just part and parcel of the scene.

BIRTH OF BE-BOP

It has been said that while early New Orleans Jazz was built on Bourbon, and 1930s' swing on marijuana, the be-bop cool of the 1940s and 1950s was fuelled by heroin. Be-bop was a revolution in jazz – it was the creation of a younger generation of black musicians seeking an identity in opposition to the mainstream – be it the white authorities or their more conventional black predecessors. Unlike earlier jazz, it made no attempt to please an audience and was not there for the entertainment of anyone but the player. Heroin is almost tailor-made for this sense of isolation. It can induce a feeling of total self-dependence (however falsely) and detachment from the world. When Charlie Parker played he really was in a world of his own – in a smacked up hermetically sealed cocoon. Jazz's love affair with heroin was assisted by the fact that most of the clubs were run by the mob and were centres for dealing.

It wasn't just heroin's ability to insulate a musician on stage that made it attractive. Being black in the USA in the first half of the twentieth century was hard at the best of times and heroin provided a solace for those off-stage as well as on. In *Soul on Ice*, Eldridge Cleaver wrote: *"Negroes found it necessary, in order to maintain what sanity they could, to remain somewhat aloof and detached from the 'problem'."* Heroin was beginning to be used more widely by the black population, but only in jazz did it reach such epidemic proportions that action had to be taken.

The number of jazz players and singers who were addicts is incalculable, but it is known to be substantial. In the 1950s, people used to joke that if you wanted to get together a top-notch band you were best off recruiting at the public health service hospitals. Why heroin became endemic among jazz players has long been a matter of dispute. Some have argued that it was just a case of younger musicians trying to emulate their heroes, such as Charlie Parker. The "Bird" was the definition of be-bop cool and idolized by a generation of younger players. Many made the mistake of thinking that he needed the heroin to play like that. He did, but only in as much as, like any addict, he needed the heroin just to get through the day – his habit was so gargantuan that he once signed over all his royalties to his dealer. But a myth was born and heroin became the drug of choice for the aspiring jazz player.

Such was the link between Parker and heroin that the first three notes of Parker's "Mood" were used as a signal by users who wanted to attract their dealer's attention. They would whistle it underneath a window. This wish to emulate heroes coupled with the easy availability of heroin on the jazz scene was at least part of the reason. Another was heroin's already well-established status as an outsider's drug. Thanks to the efforts of Hamilton Wright and Henry J. Anslinger, heroin was firmly marked down as "deviant". The new generation of black musicians, increasingly dismayed by their ostracism from society, chose to embrace the very thing that society had identified as beyond the pale. To do so was a deliberate act of rebellion, an act of defiance against people who might buy their records but never sit in a restaurant with them. As Archie Shepp once said: *"The only jazz has come out of oppression and drug addiction."*

JAZZMAN'S PLAGUE

Unfortunately, when you're talking about heroin, what starts out as a lifestyle "choice" soon becomes a necessity. As Parker himself pointed out: *"They can get it out of your blood but they can't get it out of your mind."* Before long, heroin use was being recognized as a major problem within the jazz community. Cab Calloway wrote in *Ebony* magazine in 1951 that *"A spectre is haunting the American music industry,* [it is] *the spectre of narcotics, destroying the talents of many of our finest performers, breaking up some of our best bands."* He continued in a style that Anslinger himself would have been proud of:

"Am I overstating the dope menace in music? I think not. As a practising musician for over 20 years, I know the situation as intimately as most members of our profession. I have watched an entire generation of American jazzmen develop during my career and I have seen scores of these promising artists struck down by an evil that is as cruel and relentless as a deep-sea octopus. Some of my dearest friends have been trapped by this insidious habit, which has fastened itself upon them like a plague... Drugs have caused a disturbing number of good musicians to deteriorate into hopeless has-beens. Many a fine musician who has switched to heroin to get 'turned on', has discovered to his agony that his entire creative life has been stopped cold by a terrible habit which he cannot control."

The difference between Calloway's position and that of Anslinger was that the jazz veteran was genuinely concerned for the welfare of his colleagues and their ability to continue to produce great music. He was no subscriber to the "heroin makes good music" school of thought. He was right to be alarmed – within a few years Charlie Parker was dead, at the age of thirty-five. Hampton Hawes, a musician and addict of the time wrote this in his autobiography: *"The casualty list in the fifties – dead, wounded and mentally deranged – started to look like the Korean war was being fought at the corner of Central and 45th."*

Such was the problem that, at the Newport Jazz festival in 1957, a panel discussion entitled "Music and the use of habituating drugs" was held. Its main result was the establishment of a free clinic for addicted jazz musicians in New York. That this was necessary was shown by a 1961 survey which found that within New York at least 16 per cent of jazz musicians were addicts, and more still regular users. The clinic had a good success rate in cleaning up addicted jazz musicians. Unfortunately, only a tiny fraction of New York's jazz addict fraternity ever came through the clinic's doors, which left plenty of others still out there, struggling with the "monkey on their back".

WHITE POWDER FOR A BLUE LADY

One such was Billie "Lady Day" Holiday. She had no romantic notions about heroin. *"If you think dope is for kicks and thrills you're out of your mind... if you think you need stuff to play music or sing, you're crazy. It can fix you so you can't play nothing or sing nothing."* She used it only to dull the pain. Born Eleanora Fagan in 1915 in Baltimore, Maryland, Holiday was the daughter of a guitarist. At the age of ten she was sent to reform school for "enticing" the man who had raped her. From there she went to work in a brothel, (either running errands, if you believe the sanitized version, or as a prostitute, if you take a more cynical view) which is where she first became acquainted with jazz music. By 1933 she was a star, singing in clubs all over the USA, though still being refused service in diners. In 1937, her father died of pneumonia, thinking he could not receive hospital treatment because he was black. Tired, emotionally drained and plain fed up with the crap she had to put up with on the road – as she once put it, *"It's like they say, there's no damn business like show business. You had to smile to keep from throwing up"* – she turned to heroin.

From then on her life became a series of run-ins with the law and disastrous marriages. In 1959, she collapsed in a coma for reasons that have been variously explained as cirrhosis of the liver, kidney failure, cardiac arrest or heroin but was on the road to recovery when the police raided her hospital room. There they "found" a small packet of heroin and put her under arrest. As she couldn't be moved from the hospital, the police posted armed guards at her door. Exhausted from years of drink and drug abuse and humiliated by this latest indignity, she finally gave up and died, aged forty-five.

Anita O'Day, a fellow jazz singer and heroin addict, said this of Holiday: *"I wasn't only in awe of her singing. I was in awe of her habit. She didn't cook up with a spoon. Man, she used a small tuna fish can and shot 10cc into her feet. Later I understand she ran out of veins all over her body. So she used those on either side of her vagina. One sure thing, no narc was going to bust her for fresh track marks."* Holiday's life was tragic enough without the intervention of Anslinger's heavy men. But the FBN, ever keen to be seen to be doing its job, liked to bust big-name jazz stars and Holiday was one of the biggest. She put her own case forward in her 1956 autobiography (which earned her another bust):

"People on drugs are sick people. So now we end up with the Government

BILLIE HOLIDAY HATED HER HABIT

chasing sick people like they were criminals, telling doctors they can't help them, prosecuting them because they had some stuff without paying tax and sending them to jail.

"Imagine if the Government chased sick people with diabetes, put a tax on insulin and drove it on to the black market, told doctors they couldn't treat them, and then sent them to jail. If we did that, everyone would know we were crazy. Yet we do practically the same thing every day in the week to sick people hooked on drugs. The jails are full and the problem is getting worse every day."

Anslinger's campaign against jazz musicians fulfilled the duel purpose of demonstrating that the Bureau was doing its job and appeasing Anslinger's personal distaste for jazz music. In 1949, in a report to the Ways and Means Committee, he tried to finger the jazz community for the "spread" of marijuana (another of his pet theories). "I think the traffic has increased in marijuana, and unfortunately especially among the young people. We have been running into a lot of traffic among these jazz musicians, and I am not speaking about the good musicians, but the jazz type." Anslinger's distinction between "good" music and "jazz" only served to alienate not just jazz musicians but a whole section of society, who knew a dinosaur when they saw one.

Another of Anslinger's regular victims was Chet Baker. Plucked from relative obscurity at the age of twenty-two to play with Charlie Parker, he was addicted to heroin within four years. By 1959 he had been busted seven times – surely some kind of record. He said of his regular meetings with the judiciary in an interview in 1964: "It just seemed like a field day for the police department whenever Chet Baker came to town. It seemed to be a tie-up between the police department and the newspapers."

In 1959, having lost his New York cabaret card, he went to Europe, hoping that the authorities might be less aggressive there. Unfortunately, he underestimated the determination of that continent's judiciary to keep itself clean and spent time in prison in both Britain and Italy. Baker was always bigger in Europe than in the USA and spent the last thirteen years of his life there, dying in somewhat mysterious circumstances in 1988 – having fallen out of a window in Amsterdam.

THE BEAT WRITERS

The jazz of the 1940s and 1950s was hugely influential on later music and its legacy of drug taking would resurface regularly over the following decades. But be-bop was influential in another area – that of the beat writers. They ransacked be-bop not just for its rhythmic style, but also its practitioners' lifestyle. The beat poets were almost adolescent in their

reverence for the great jazz junkies like Charlie Parker.

The most famous beat writers are now Jack Kerouac, Allen Ginsberg and William Burroughs. These three met at Columbia University in New York in the 1940s and stayed in contact for the rest of their lives, encouraging one another both in their literary endeavours and in their narcotic appetites. The beat poets were the self-proclaimed representatives of the "beat generation", a term first coined in 1948 by Jack Kerouac but explained to the world in an article for the *New York Times Magazine* in 1952 by John Clellon Holmes, another beat writer.

Holmes was prompted to write the article by the arrest of an 18-year-old Californian girl for smoking marijuana. The case had received much publicity along the lines of "the youth of today, where's it all going to end?" In his article, called "This is the Beat Generation", Holmes described a generation who had been born into the Great Depression of the 1930s, whose childhood had been lived under the shadow of the Second World War, who knew of the extremes of Hitler on the one hand and Stalin on the other, whose fathers or brothers had been killed and who were now living under the shadow of another, apparently unwinnable, war – a cold one. It is hardly surprising, he suggests, that this generation is "beat", in the sense of exhausted or as he put it *"the feeling of having been used, of being raw. It involves a sort of nakedness of mind, and, ultimately of soul; a feeling of being reduced to the bedrock of consciousness....Their own lust for freedom, and the ability to live at a pace that kills (to which the war had adjusted them), led to black markets, be-bop, narcotics, sexual promiscuity, hucksterism, and Jean-Paul Sartre."*

Holmes' beat generation is essentially any teenage generation going through the usual dynamic of rejecting the mores of their parents and their rulers. But where they differed from, for example, the "flapper" generation that came after the First World War (with whom Holmes compares them) is in their experimentation with sex and drugs – he talks of the "...wildest hipster, making a mystique of bop, drugs and night-life."

Kerouac later turned this definition of beat on its head, claiming that it meant *"beatitude, not beat up. You feel this. You feel it in a beat, in jazz realcool jazz."* For Kerouac, be-bop jazz was the ultimate paradigm for beat writing, and jazzmen the icons of the beat generation. There is a clear link between the stylistic qualities of be-bop and the beat writers. In a 1968 interview, Allen Ginsberg said: *"Kerouac learned his line from Charlie Parker, and Gillespie, and Monk. He was listening in '43 to Symphony Sid and listening to 'Night in Tunisia' and all the Bird-flight-noted things which he then adapted to prose line."* Beat writers borrowed a lot of their language from jazz: apart from beat, there was "square", "cats", "nowhere" and "dig", which are all jazz/beat terms.

You can hear be-bop in Allen Ginsberg's most famous poem, "Howl". He first claimed that it was based on a Charlie Parker song but later changed his mind, claiming that *"Lester Young, actually, is what I was thinking about... Howl is all 'Lester leaps in'. And I got that from Kerouac. Or paid attention to it on account of Kerouac, surely – he made me listen to it."*

But it wasn't just the formal qualities of jazz music that inspired the beat writers. It was also the lifestyle. They idolized their jazz heroes as much for their drug-taking as for any influence they might have had on their literary style. John Clellon Holmes, though, unusually for the beat writers, having no particular taste for jazz, wrote a novel *The Horn* whose central characters, Geordie and Edgar Pool, were based on Billie Holiday and Charlie Parker respectively.

As John Arthur Maynard wrote in his 1991 book *Venice West*:

"Jazz served as the ultimate point of reference, even though, or perhaps even because, few among them played it. From it they adopted the mythos of the brooding, tortured, solitary artist, performing with

others but always alone. They talked the talk of jazz, built communal rites around using the jazzman's drugs, and worshipped the dead jazz musicians most fervently. The musician whose music was fatal represented pure spontaneity."

The beat generation used drugs to demonstrate their marginality. Henry J. Anslinger and friends had done such a good job of demonizing heroin that taking it embraced a full-scale attack on American values. While heroin was a tragic accident that happened to the Jazz world, for the beat generation it was an act of will.

Clellon Holmes wrote: *"In this modern jazz, they heard something rebel and nameless that spoke for them, and their lives knew a gospel for the first time. It was more than a music; it became an attitude toward life, a way of walking, a language and a costume; and these introverted kids... now felt somewhere at last."*

All the beat writers experimented with drugs – it was a signal of their "otherness". The opening lines of Allen Ginsberg's "Howl" are:
"I saw the best minds of my generation destroyed by
madness, starving hysterical naked
Dragging themselves through the negro streets at dawn
looking for an angry fix."

When Ginsberg went to London, he was championed by Dame Edith Sitwell. The Grande Dame of English poetry and eccentric hats took Ginsberg and his companion, fellow beat author Gregory Corso, to lunch at her club, the Sesame. When he offered her some heroin, the 71-year-old author of the experimental poem *Façade* declined, explaining *"it brings me out in spots"*.

In order to affirm their outsider status, the beat writers hung out with low-lifes and junkies. Of these there were plenty in the New York jazz clubs they frequented such as the Red Drum, Minton's and the Open Door. One of the crooks they most lionized was Herbert Huncke, who found his way into Kerouac's and Burroughs' fiction and Ginsberg's flat.

Huncke was a small-time crook who had the good luck to have a surname that rhymed with junkie. He started doing drugs at the age of twelve and within four years was working as a runner for Al Capone's gang in Chicago. After that he drifted round America, robbing and hustling (though he claimed to be a very poor prostitute – *"I was always falling in love,"* he once said). He came to New York in 1939 and set up operations peddling drugs and anything else, including his body. It was in 1945 that he met William Burroughs, whom he introduced to heroin. The meeting is recorded in Burroughs' autobiographical novel *Junky* (in which Huncke appears as "Herman"):

"Waves of hostility and suspicion flowed out from his large brown eyes like some sort of television broadcast. The effect was almost like a physical impact. The man was small and very thin, his neck loose in the collar of his shirt. His complexion faded from brown to a mottled yellow, and pancake make-up had been heavily applied in an attempt to conceal a skin eruption. His mouth was drawn down at the corners in a grimace of petulant annoyance."

Burroughs had gone there to sell a gun that had come his way. Huncke/Herman was the proposed buyer. Burroughs introduced Huncke to Jack Kerouac and Allen Ginsberg. The latter invited Huncke to live with him and included him in his poem "Howl", with its reference to *"Huncke's bloody feet"*. Kerouac wrote of him adoringly in *On the road*, in which he is "Elmer Hassel", and in John Clellon Holmes' only successful novel *Go* Huncke appears as "Ancke". In addition, he supposedly inspired Kerouac to come up with the term "beat", through his repeated use of it. If Charlie Parker was the "black godfather" of the beat generation, Huncke was its white one.

Huncke, influenced by his new friends, took up writing as well – working in a men's toilet cubicle on the New York subway. His work, however, has never achieved much recognition. His real claim to fame is his legend as immortalized in the works of the beat writers. He lived the life they romanticized, remaining a heroin addict throughout his life, much of which he spent in prison. In his later years, he was supported by friends and admirers, notably that other famous junkie, Jerry Garcia of the Grateful Dead. He died at the Chelsea hotel in 1996, aged eighty-one.

THE JUNKY'S TALE

Whether or not William Burroughs liked jazz is open to question, but he certainly liked heroin. Born in 1914 in Missouri, Burroughs was from a well-to-do middle-class family which remained a source of embarrassment to him, except for when he claimed his monthly trust fund cheque. He was either the natural heir to Jonathan Swift (according to Mary McCarthy) or the purveyor of "bogus high-brow filth" (according to Victor Gollancz). Nor did Edith Sitwell, who championed his friend Allen Ginsberg, take to him. *"I do not wish to spend the rest of my life with my nose nailed to other people's lavatories,"* she wrote. *"I prefer Chanel No 5."*

Having been introduced to heroin by Huncke in 1945, Burroughs spent the next fifteen years devoting himself and his trust fund to it. After the war he moved to Mexico, where he started writing *Junky*, under the pseudonym William Lee. *Junky*'s title is self-explanatory. It tells the more or less autobiographical story of Lee/Burroughs' hand-to-mouth existence in New York and Mexico. It details the day-to-day life of an addict and the "etiquette" and language of the world of heroin – the constant running from the police, the agonies of withdrawal, in short, the desperate minutiae of that strange other world inhabited by the junkie. It is at the same time dull – an addict's life is, as Burroughs is prepared to admit – and fascinating.

While in Mexico, Burroughs shot his wife, Joan. Apparently they had been playing "William Tell", his wife taking the part of the son and William that of the famous archer, although substituting a glass for the apple and using a gun in place of a bow and arrow. Unfortunately for Joan, Burroughs was no William Tell and she was shot dead. Luckily for Burroughs, the police believed him and he was never charged. He left Mexico and travelled around South America experimenting with drugs till the late 1950s, when he settled in

WILLIAM BURROUGHS RAISED HEROIN TO THE STATE OF ART

Tangier, along with his drug habit, which he called his "old friend opium Jones." Describing his life there he wrote:

"We were mighty close in Tangier in 1957, shooting every hour 15 grains of methadone per day which equals 30 grains of morphine and that's a lot of GOM [God's own medicine].

"I never changed my clothes. Jones likes his clothes to season in stale rooming-house flesh until you can tell by a hat on the table, a coat hung over a chair that Jones lives there. I never took a bath. Old Jones don't like the feel of water on his skin.

"I spent whole days looking at the end of my shoe just communing with Jones. Then one day I saw that Jones was not a real friend, that our interests were in fact divergent. So I took a plane to London and found Doctor Dent."

Dr Dent was the man who weaned Burroughs off heroin, prescribing apomorphine. Burroughs had tried to come off heroin several times before (he details some of these failed attempts in *Junky*). He had a particular contempt for the use of methadone to cure an addict, saying that it was like giving gin to someone addicted to whisky in order to break the habit. But Dr Dent succeeded where all others had failed and Burroughs made sure he got a credit in all his books from then on. Burroughs never went back to heroin and, despite future generations hailing him as a heroin hero, he criticized his former habit. In his introduction to *Naked Lunch*, he writes:

"I awoke from the sickness at the age of forty-five, calm and sane, and in reasonably good health except for a weakened liver and the look of borrowed flesh common to all who survive the sickness."

Many have seen Burroughs as an apologist for heroin but his introduction to *Naked Lunch* makes it clear that he is not apologizing for his past life:

"I have seen the exact manner in which the junk virus operates through fifteen years of addiction," he wrote. *"Junk is the mold of monopoly and possession... Junk is the ideal product... the ultimate merchandise. No sales talk necessary. The client will crawl through a sewer and beg to buy.... The junk merchant... degrades and simplifies the client."*

He ends the introduction with this warning: *"Look down LOOK DOWN along that junk road before you travel there and get in with the wrong mob.... A word to the wise guy."* Hardly a romantic paean to the joys of heroin addiction, and one his son clearly paid no attention to, dying in 1981 after years of drug addiction and alcoholism.

Burroughs lived to the impressive age of eighty-three, dying in 1997, the same year as Ginsberg. He has remained an iconographic figure as much for his supposed devotion to heroin as his literature – in 1992

Kurt Cobain released an album with him called "The Priest They Called Him", with Cobain on guitar while Burroughs reads.

ROCK AND GRUNGE

Jazz was the first musical movement to embrace heroin – but not the last. While there have always been musicians who have taken heroin, just as there have always been accountants and lawyers who do, the drug is associated most with two other periods in the history of music – the rock of the late 1960s/early 1970s and the grunge of the late 1980s. Leading the pack and setting the standard for everyone to follow were the Velvet Underground.

The Velvet Underground were formed in 1966, taking their name from the title of a German sado-masochistic novel someone found lying around. Comprising Lou Reed on vocals, John Cale on keyboard and the androgenous Maureen Tucker on drums, they changed rock music for ever. Andy Warhol soon got wind of them, insisting they add the mysterious Nico to their line-up, and decided to put them in a travelling show called the "Exploding Plastic Inevitable", for reasons that remain mysterious but most likely had something to do with drugs. The show was a hit, combining controversial lyrics and even more controversial visuals.

While music in the past may have referred to drugs indirectly, the Velvet Underground were upfront. In songs such as "Waiting for the Man" and "Heroin" there was no room for ambiguity about the principal theme. Just in case you didn't get it, while Reed sang *"Heroin will be the death of me, but it's my wife and it's my life,"* a dancer called Gerard Malanga would go through the ritual of shooting-up on stage, heating a spoon, injecting himself and then collapsing coma-like.

There is some debate as to whether or not Lou Reed ever took heroin. He once said *"just because I write about it doesn't mean I do it."* It's quite possibly true – in his solo album *Transformer* he adopted the persona of a transvestite but people have generally recognized that for the conceit that it was. Reed, like the beat writers, was using heroin for its unparalleled metaphorical power. Unlike them, it's quite possible he was able to leave it at that. Others, however, were not. On the whole, heroin's use in music has been actual, rather than metaphorical. Often with tragic endings.

The Velvet Underground didn't last long – Nico left in 1967, in a heroin haze that she was to remain in for the next 20 years, Cale left in 1969 and Reed in 1970 – but their legacy was seen in the glam rock and punk of the 1970s. The Velvet Underground's immediate successors were the New York Dolls, who stole much of the look without managing to recapture the extraordinary sound. They took the Velvet Underground's sexual androgyny and took it that one step further, giving the world "glam rock" as it came to be known. They also took Lou Reed's words at face value, knocking back drugs like they were going out of fashion. They even replicated Gerard Malanga's shooting-up routine on stage when they sang "Looking for a Kiss". Back stage, unlike Reed, they were doing it for real:

"This was the first time we saw drugs kill a band," said a member of another band, Aerosmith, talking of the Dolls, *"Their first drummer had OD'd in London. Johnny Thunders was a heroin addict who was always shooting up in the back of wherever we were. He'd trade his guitar for drugs when he ran out, and I kept thinking, Boy, that'll never happen to us.... They'd cancel gigs when they ran out of drugs, fly back to New York and score. Seven days on the road was all they could do because they'd get sick. We'd hear that Johnny and the drummer had to go back to New York because they were 'tired'. Yeah, right."*

Johnny Thunders eventually died of his addiction in 1991. Aerosmith had little reason to feel smug – Steve Tyler and Joe Perry, respectively singer and guitarist with the band, earned the nickname the "toxic twins" in the 1970s, such was their capacity for drug taking. Perry, who started taking heroin in the mid 1970s, said that his main recollection of recording the band's 1977 album, "Draw the Line" was *"this huge bottle of Tuinals which I hid under the sink"*. The band were in such a state that they sometimes played the same song twice by mistake in a live show. They never left the USA to tour in Europe, for fear of being caught by customs. Aerosmith were teetering perilously close to the edge and looked like they were going to the Rock cemetery with so many of their predecessors when someone persuaded them to take part in a drug rehabilitation programme – which, in all, took about four years. They emerged, free of drugs, and remain hugely successful.

Sadly, Aerosmith's return from the brink is hardly typical. A twelve-month period, from 1970-1971, saw three of the greatest rock singers of all time die in heroin-related deaths. First was Jimi Hendrix, who died in 1970 from a barbiturate overdose. A few weeks later, his death was followed by Janis Joplin's, from a lethal cocktail of tequila and heroin. Joplin, who stunned the audience when she appeared as an unknown at the notorious Monterey pop festival in 1967, had no concept of moderation. In retrospect, she is a stereotypical student of the "live fast, die young" school of rock music, announcing shortly before she died: *"I wanted to smoke dope, take dope, lick dope, suck dope and fuck dope."*

Within a year of Joplin's death, Jim Morrison, lead vocalist of the Doors, had died in his bath. The exact cause of his death remains a mystery –

it was reported as a heart attack, but only his wife and an unidentified doctor ever saw the body before its burial at Père Lachaise cemetery in Paris. The rumour mill has been in overdrive ever since, particularly as his widow died of a heroin overdose in 1975 and is thus unable to clear up the mystery. The most commonly suggested theory is that Morrison was put in the bath in an attempt to revive him from a heroin overdose.

In 1973, Gram Parsons, who effectively invented the genre of country/rock, was found dead in his hotel room. Parsons left a small output from his brief career but a huge legacy and, like all good rock stars, a mystery surrounding his death. His manager, apparently acting in accordance with Parson's wishes, stole his body *en route* to the funeral and burnt it in the Mojave desert. Needless to say, tongues have been wagging ever since.

Heroin took a sabbatical from the world of music through the late seventies and eighties (not counting Sid Vicious). It wasn't exactly a disco drug. But it came back with a vengeance with the arrival of grunge.

SEATTLE SOUNDS

Grunge came from the suburbs of Seattle and (for some) provided a much needed antidote to the excesses of the 1980s. A direct challenge to the plastic pop coming predominantly from the UK, Grunge was raw where the New Romantics and their descendants were over-dressed, over-produced and altogether artificial. Grunge was recession rock and the first musical movement since punk that seemed to be making a full on attack on society.

As before, rebellion meant that the ultimate icon of deviance – heroin – took centre stage. The artists of grunge felt disenfranchized, just as the jazz musicians of the 1950s had been and just as the generation that saw the disaster of the Vietnam war had been. Heroin became a solace, as it had been for those previous generations, but it also became *de rigeur*. And once again the deaths began to mount up: Andrew Wood, of Mother Love Bone in 1990, Stefanie Sargent, of 7 Year Bitch in 1993, Kurt Cobain's suicide in 1994 and Kristen Pfaff, of Hole, also in 1994. In 1995, Everclear, another grunge rock band, released "Heroin Girl". Since then, music has taken one of its periodic breaks from heroin. Doubtless it will return when a new generation needs to articulate its frustration.

SCANDALS

HOLLYWOOD HIGHS

Right from the start, the story of heroin has been accompanied by scandal. First came Hollywood, starting as it meant to go on. In 1922, matinée idol Wallace Reid, the "king of Paramount", was sent to a sanatorium by his studio. The official excuse was that old standby "overwork" but his wife, herself an actor, let the papers know the real reason – addiction. Reid's committal was as shocking as Rock Hudson's admission that he had AIDS some sixty years later. Reid was the archetypal blue-eyed all-American hero of crowd-pleasing films such as *The Roaring Road* and *What's Your Hurry?* Suddenly, the USA was awake to the fact that there was something rotten at the core of Hollywood. Reid died just one year after his admittance to the sanatorium, which he never left.

Hollywood tried to make the best of a bad job by casting his wife in *Human Wreckage*, trailed as *"the greatest production in the history of motion pictures"* and a film that is *"endorsed by the biggest list of the biggest and best organizations and individuals in the country – it is being backed by a colossal campaign that will soon reach unprecedented proportions – it will be the centre of tremendously important and vital national events."*

Preceding the film action was a short but no less insistent message: *"Dope is the gravest menace which today confronts the United States. Immense quantities of morphine, heroin and cocaine are yearly smuggled into America"* Quite a lot of this annual import, it seemed, going straight to Hollywood.

Reid was the first in a series of silent stars whose addictions became public along with their downfall. Next was Barbara La Marr, the "girl who was too beautiful". La Marr managed to make nearly thirty films and have five husbands by the time of her death at the age of twenty-nine. She once explained how she managed to pack all this activity in to her life saying: *"I cheat nature. I never sleep more than two hours a day. I have better things to do – I take lovers like roses, by the dozen!"* What she failed to mention was that there was nothing natural about her "cheating of nature". During the filming of *Souls for Sale* in 1923, La Marr had started using morphine and heroin, helpfully provided by a studio "doctor" after she injured herself on set. Soon, she was addicted and, within three years, she was dead.

Heroin made an unwelcome return to Hollywood in the 1990s, with the death of River Phoenix. River Jude Phoenix was born in Madras in 1970. The name "River" came from the "River of Life", taken from Hermann Hesse's mystical novel *Siddharta*. His parents,

LIFE IMITATES ART - RIVER PHOENIX IN MY OWN PRIVATE IDAHO

John Bottom and Arlyn Dunetz, were members of a cult known as the "Children of God". They considered themselves to be missionaries, their mission being to recruit as many new members as possible to the cult. River was actually quite lucky, as far as names went – the rest of his family were named Rain Joan of Arc, Joaquin Raphael, Libertad Mariposa (Liberty Butterfly) and Summer Joy. When the Children of God collapsed in some ignominy, the family rechristened themselves Phoenix, after the mythological bird that rises from the ashes of its own destruction.

Phoenix was a hugely talented actor who looked set to become one of the greats of his generation. In *My Own Private Idaho* (1991) he knocked spots off of the main box office draw in the film, Keanu Reeves. Phoenix played "Mike", a male prostitute who was in love with the character played by Reeves. It was during the filming of this movie that Phoenix started getting heavily into drugs.

In the early hours of October 31, 1993, Phoenix was at Johnny Depp's night-club, The Viper Room, in Los Angeles, with Rain, Joaquin, and his girlfriend, Samantha Mathis. Just before midnight, he began to suffer seizures. He slumped down and slid under the table. He said he couldn't breathe and needed air. Joaquin and Rain dragged him to the nearest exit. As they made their way past the stage, River called out, *"Hey Dude, I've done a speed ball. I'm going to die."* And he did, at 1.51 am, from an overdose of cocaine and heroin. The cocaine present was eight times the lethal dose. Phoenix's death shocked the world, not only because of his youth (he was twenty-three) and talent but because he had always projected a clean-living image. He was a vegetarian and animal rights campaigner – hardly the sort of hell-raising image normally associated with drug deaths.

MUSICAL LOWS

Henry Anslinger's habit of busting big-name jazz musicians proved popular with succeeding law enforcement officers. The press, too, always liked a juicy drug scandal. So, when a new generation of musician drug users came into the spotlight in the 1960s and 1970s, the forces of law and order and the fourth estate were right on their heels. No one's more so than the Rolling Stones', especially Keith Richards'. The Stones' rocky relationship with the police started in 1967, at the infamous "Mars Bar party" at Richards' country estate, Redlands, in South-east England. At the house, along with Keith Richards, were Mick Jagger, Marianne Faithful, Anita Pallenberg, George and Patti Harrison and art dealer and friend to the stars Robert Fraser. The Harrisons had already left when the police raided, but the rest were searched and booked. Richards was initially sentenced to a

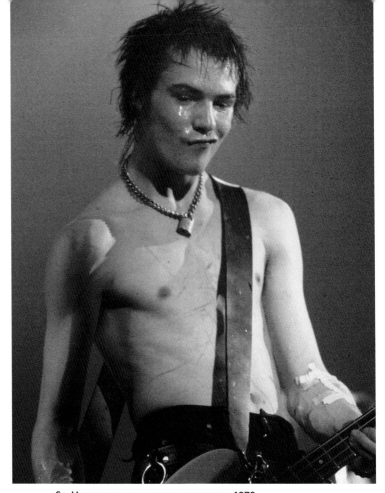

SID VICIOUS DIED OF A HEROIN OVERDOSE IN 1979

year in prison for allowing drugs to be taken in his house (a curious British law dating from the 1920s) and Jagger to three months for possession of amphetamine. Robert Fraser, who was found in possession of heroin, got six months. However, Richards' conviction was subsequently quashed on appeal and Jagger's reduced to a conditional discharge.

This was the Stones' first of many forays into the law courts and it also established the British press's approach to such stories. The whole affair was printed in lurid detail, the downmarket papers paying particular attention to the more exotic aspects of the case, particularly the "sexual" role that the Mars Bar played in the proceedings – one that probably existed only in the fevered imagination of a prurient news hound. The upmarket papers moralized long and hard on the use of drugs in contemporary popular music and the deleterious effect it was having on the nation's youth. Neither side of the newspaper spectrum has seen any reason to change their position since.

But while Jagger may have been the frontman on stage, Richards was always the main performer in the law courts. He has become a living (in itself a remarkable feat) legend in the world of heroin, generating rumour and fascination in equal measure. His most serious brush with the authorities was in 1977, in Toronto. Anita Pallenberg, his "common law wife" was arrested at the airport and Richards, a few days later, in his hotel room. He was found in possession of a substantial amount of heroin and charged with being in possession with intent to supply. However, he was able to convince the court that the large quantity was just for him – almost certainly true given his, by then, considerable habit – and was found guilty only of the lesser charge of possession. He was put on probation and ordered to play a concert for the blind.

Others took on Richards' mantle over the following decades. First Sid Vicious in the 1970s and then Boy George in the 1980s. Both celebrities had been emblematic of their age but were past the heyday of their popularity when scandal broke. The press like nothing better than to kick a star when he's down. For Sid Vicious there was no comeback, his messy life and death immortalized in the film *Sid and Nancy* (1986). Boy George achieved the seemingly impossible, returning from heroin oblivion to some degree of respectability as a DJ, sometime recording artist and even newspaper columnist for the papers that had so hounded him in his darkest days.

HEROIN ON CELLULOID

All of a sudden, seemingly out of nowhere, heroin made a comeback in the 1990s. The music, film and fashion industries just couldn't get enough of it (metaphorically – there is no evidence that they ever had any actual problems getting hold of heroin). Politicians and the media were quick to enter the fray and for the first time since the seventies heroin became the drug you loved to hate.

First up for censure was Hollywood, which "glamorized" the drug in a clutch of films. Gus Van Sant and Quentin Tarantino came in for the worst of the criticism, each with two heroin-related films to their credit. Van Sant's *Drugstore Cowboy* (1989) followed a group of desperate addicts on the run from the police, robbing pharmacies *en route*. It even featured a cameo performance from William Burroughs. *My Own Private Idaho* , based very, very loosely on Shakespeare's *Henry IV Part 2*, told the story of two male hustlers, played by

Keanu Reeves and River Phoenix. In neither film could Van Sant be said to have glamorized heroin; in *Drugstore Cowboy* the life depicted was one of desperation, resolved only by the decision of the main character (played by Matt Dillon) to go straight at the end. In *My Own Private Idaho*, the doomed junkie, River Phoenix's character, is in sharp contrast to Keanu Reeves' self-assured good-time boy. Phoenix dies, Reeves inherits his father's money and goes straight.

Tarantino's *Pulp Fiction* (1994) tells the interweaving stories of a group of low-lifers – hit men, drug dealers, armed robbers and so on. It is an exercise in style as much as anything, shot in almost cartoon-like colour, with often surreal dialogue. *Pulp Fiction* uses heroin as many films have done – as a symbol for gangsterism, but knowingly. Such is heroin's outlaw status that if you ever need to indicate that someone is beyond the pale you simply show him or her taking or dealing in heroin. It's a movie short-cut. Films have repeatedly used this device, with varying degrees of sophistication. Just as Westerns used to dress the bad guy all in black, nowadays the bad guy takes heroin.

In *Pulp Fiction*, heroin is just one of the film "sign-posts" that Tarantino explores. The film also features violence (lots), sado-masochism and homosexual rape. What offended many is that the film is very funny, often even camp. But Tarantino is effectively parodying the use of these stereotypical film short-cuts and the laziness of other film-makers in using them. The film also asks its

DRUGSTORE COWBOY, IN WHICH MATT DILLON GOES STRAIGHT

audience why these things are so shocking – is it just that we have been so bombarded by politicians and the media with images of devastation that we are no longer able to think for ourselves?

Other films singled out for their depiction of heroin use were *The Basketball Diaries*, made (1995) and starring Leonardo de Caprio as a strung-out heroin addict, and *Trainspotting* (1995). The latter was perhaps the most controversial of the lot. Set in an Edinburgh far removed from its traditional image as the Athens of the North, *Trainspotting* is the story of five friends – all addicts.

The film charts the inevitable collapse of the characters' lives as they lurch from one disaster to another, often very funnily. It was this last attribute that offended people – the idea that heroin could be in any way humorous. Nor did the film shy away from describing the pleasures of taking heroin – not what the drug educators wanted to hear. *Trainspotting* was a surprise hit, gaining an Academy Award nomination for best adapted script and raking it in at the box office both in Europe and the USA (despite the incomprehensible working-class Scots accents of the cast).

HEROIN CHIC

It wasn't just films that were apparently buying into heroin. Fashion too, on one of its periodic whims, had decided that heroin was cool. Or at least people who looked as if they were on heroin were cool. A group of fashion stylists and photographers, drawing on the work of seminal 1980s photographer Nan Goldin, created "heroin chic". Heroin chic aimed to get away from the traditional glamour shots of Vogue and Harpers Bazaar. Instead, it showed models who looked painfully thin, tired and – not to put too fine a point on it – junked up. Stylists even took to spraying models with water to simulate that "junkie sweat" look.

The look was pioneered by Davide Sorrenti, a young New York-based photographer. In response to one of his shoots for the US magazine *Detour*, actress Juliette Lewis (who, ironically, starred in the supposedly pro-heroin film *The Basketball Diaries*) wrote a letter of complaint: *"This was the most deliberate Junkie layout I have ever seen and I don't know why this is being allowed, as it is promoting such a degraded state."* Leigh Leventhal, speaking for the Partnership for a Drug-free America in 1996, said: *"In music, film and fashion, heroin is being positioned as the drug of the Nineties."*

But what really brought heroin chic to the wider public's notice was Calvin Klein's 1996 campaign for his new fragrance, CKBe. This showed models of both sexes hunched up, hollow eyed and looking as if they hadn't had a meal in ages (even more so than usual).

Heroin and fashion hit the front pages when Davide Sorrenti, its main proponent, was found dead of a heroin overdose in 1997, aged just twenty. President Clinton, at the US Conference of Mayors later that year, laid into the fashion and entertainment industry's latest fad: *"The glorification of heroin is not creative, it's destructive. It's not beautiful, it is ugly. And this is not about art, it's about life and death."* Not to be outdone, Bob Dole, his rival in the upcoming Presidential elections came up with a new campaign slogan: *"Just don't do it."* He added *"there can be no question that the trendiest trend of our popular culture is the return of drug use... the marijuana leaf and the heroin needle have become the symbols of fashionable rebellion... Fashion magazines feature models with what is known as the 'junkie look'. Rock musicians create and celebrate a culture of heroin..."*

Dole also singled out *Trainspotting* and *Pulp Fiction*, for censure, although it later emerged that he had seen neither and had *"based his assessment on reading the reviews."* Others lined up with the White House hopefuls, threatening to boycott Klein's products: *"Addiction is neither chic nor glamorous..."* said the executive director of National Families in Action. *"Until Calvin Klein stops glamorizing heroin addiction, we refuse to buy Calvin Klein products. We are asking America's families to join us."*

Laura Craik of British style magazine *the Face* retorted to the hysteria by asserting in a 1997 interview with the *Guardian* newspaper : *"We like to believe our readers are far too intelligent to be nudged into the twilight world of drug abuse by a mere picture of a wasted-looking model. This is not to deny that art and life sometimes cross over; only that when they do, we trust that they can tell the difference between the myth of a glassy, glossy illusion and the reality behind it."*

Nevertheless, fashion did decide it needed to clean-up its act. Executive Director of the Council of Fashion Designers of America, Fern Mallis, promised: *"We understand the responsibility of being more responsible"*. But by the time any of these initiatives had got going the fashion for thin was already out and fat (up to a point) was in. Junkie models, of whom there were still plenty, no longer had the right look.

The extent to which art and life did cross over was, however, becoming more and more apparent. It began to emerge that many of the models being photographed to look like junkies actually were junkies, as one by one they checked in for "rest cures." Davide Sorrenti's mother Francesca, herself a fashion photographer, let the cat out of the bag: *"The bottom line,"* she said in response to the fashion industry's new found scruples, *"is these pictures can be smiling all they want and the girl behind the smile might be on* drugs," she said. "*Heroin chic isn't what we're projecting, it's what we are.*" Drug use could even be a positive advantage to a model – heroin-using models practised "grouching out": when a model comes round from a dope-induced faint. She has a faraway, sexy look in her eyes, perfect for that cover shot.

Francesca Sorrenti embarked on a campaign of her own, writing letters to fashion magazines and designers: "*We must clean up our own house,*" she wrote. "*It is time to take a stand against certain traditions of the fashion business. It is time to establish rules that will protect children in a profession that has no laws.*"

In the UK, thirteen leading designers responded by forming Designers Against Addiction (DAD). One of them, John Moore, of royal designers Hardy Amies, had this to say: "*The fashion industry is so influential on young people that if we can pull together to behave responsibly then only good can come of it*". DAD held a show benefit, and issued a statement vowing not to hire models who used drugs, signed by John Galliano, Stella McCartney and Bella Freud, among others.

Similar hand-wringing was seen in the music business. A spate of rock star overdoses were alarming record company executives and parents alike. It was like the 1970s all over again. In 1990, Andrew Wood, vocalist with Mother Love Bone, died of a heroin overdose. Wood liked to wear silver suits and platform-soled motorcycle boots and looked every inch the 1970s rock star. He died like one too, aged twenty-four. In 1993, Stefanie Sargent, of 7 Year Bitch, died. The next year, Kurt Cobain shot himself. He had very nearly died a week earlier from a heroin overdose and was on heroin at the time of his self-inflicted death.

Singer with Nirvana and the most important artist to emerge from the Grunge scene, Cobain and his wife Courtney Love had provided much fruit for the scandal mongers. In a feature on them in *Vanity Fair*, in 1992, it was alleged that Love had been using heroin while pregnant with the couple's daughter, Frances Bean, something the two vehemently denied. At Cobain's death, fans gathered to mourn in public in scenes of communal grief not witnessed since the shooting of John Lennon. Cobain's death was shortly followed by that of Kristen Pfaff, the bassist in Courtney Love's band Hole, from a heroin overdose. By now, the connection between grunge and heroin was firmly established in the public mind. Shannon Hoon, the lead singer of Blind Mellon, said this shortly before he too overdosed in 1995: "*Whatever route someone's going to take, they should look a little bit into it before they take that route.*"

The music industry tried, as the jazz community had 30 years earlier, to put its house in order. The National Academy of Recording Arts and Sciences (NARAS) in October 1995 held an "industry intervention" in Santa Monica. Various record company executives and assorted industry affiliates met to discuss how best to solve the problem, concluding that they needed to *"stop brushing the problems under the table"*.

Less generous souls suspected the industry's motives – Robert Smith of the Cure for one. *"I'm afraid it's just some kind of goodwill gesture made for publicity purposes,"* he said. *"Record companies and people in the business have always been some of the most tight-fisted, self-centred people in the world... I've found they're not really interested in helping musicians with problems, because if someone falls by the wayside they can usually find someone else to help them make money."*

He might have added that any inconvenience generated by the death of a major star tends to be offset by huge posthumous record sales. Another singer, Mojo Nixon, was even more derisive. *"It's ludicrous,"* he said of the whole furore. *"No one's going to do anything. It's like the military saying we're not going to be violent... or like politicians saying we're not going to lie."*

It seemed he was right as the deaths piled up. Jonathan Melvoin, keyboard player with the Smashing Pumpkins, died in July 1996. With typical perversity, New York addicts were desperate to lay their hands on "Red Rum", the super-strong brand of heroin on which he had overdosed. The group's drummer, Jimmy Chamberlain, was with him at the time and the group promptly replaced him. Some had lucky escapes, notably David Gahan, the singer with British group Depeche Mode. After a near fatal overdose in 1996, he became an unlikely convert to the anti-drugs crusade: *"All I can do is hope my actions will speak much louder than the crap that's come out of my mouth the last few years,"* he said from the treatment centre his record company had demanded he attend. *"When I think about the insanity of this little powder – three minutes of euphoria,"* he continued, *"you don't have to be a lifetime user. It only takes one time. People seem to believe the myth that if you just do it once you're fine, and now many people seem to be going straight to heroin, bypassing pot and all that and going straight to the devil. It's really scary."*

One of Gahan's contemporaries who did go "straight to the devil" was Michael Hutchence. Hutchence, the lead singer with Australian group INXS, was in his own words, *"bloody good at being a rock star"*. By the criteria of the profession this was true. He consumed Herculean quantities of drugs and alcohol, drove a motorcycle and an Aston Martin, had a villa near Nice, dabbled in the films, punched photographers and had superstar girlfriends including Kylie Minogue,

Helena Christiansen and Paula Yates (with whom he had a daughter, Heavenly Hiraani Tiger Lily). Hutchence was found hanging by a belt around his neck from a hotel doorway, naked. The press immediately seized upon this as a sign that he had been engaged in auto-erotic asphyxiation at the time, although the coroner subsequently ruled that he had hanged himself intentionally. At the autopsy, Hutchence's body was found to be awash with narcotic substances; he had once said: *"The good, sensible, rock and roll thing to do is to be completely drunk, take drugs and have sex all day."* This was perhaps an unwise statement to make in view of the ugly custody battle Paula Yates was involved in at the time with her ex-husband Bob Geldof.

HIGH SOCIETY

The sons and daughters of the British upper classes have long had a fondness for heroin – for some reason heroin, like horse racing, crosses class barriers in the UK.

In June, 1986, the British papers were filled with news of the death of a student at Oxford university, Olivia Channon. She had died of a heroin overdose taken at a party held to celebrate the end of her exams. What made Olivia Channon's death newsworthy was the fact that her father was a minister in Margaret Thatcher's Government. She had been partying with a group of friends whose surnames were familiar to any reader of society columns, including the great-great-grandson of Otto von Bismarck, the "Iron Chancellor" of Germany. The press had a field day, "exposing" the decadent lifestyles of students at one of Britain's top universities.

In the 1990s, the British papers once again revelled in drug scandal, this time involving Charles Tennant, son and heir of Lord Glenconner, a close friend of the Queen's sister Princess Margaret. Tennant had started taking LSD in the 1960s and then moved on to opiates to calm himself down. Like many of his upbringing, heroin was the ultimate rebellion: *"It was a down and out desperado's drug,"* he later said. *"There was an appeal in that alone."*

In 1978, he achieved notoriety by stealing from his mother some personal photos of Princess Margaret, which he sold to his dealer for a quarter of a gram of heroin. His dealer sold them on to a national newspaper for considerably more. His mother did at least get her own back by suing the paper for breach of copyright and forcing them to pay a substantial sum to a charity for recovering drug addicts.

Tennant recovered from his heroin addiction but in 1996 died of hepatitis C, contracted through sharing needles while an addict. His younger brother Henry had already died of HIV in 1990, contracted the same way.

The most colourful of Britain's heroin aristocrats was the Marquis of Bristol, who finally died in 1999 aged forty-four, his body exhausted from the cumulative effects of drink and drug abuse. He had been providing "copy" for the British press for decades – indeed his ever-eccentric family had itself been providing all-round merriment since the eighteenth century. At the age of sixteen, the Marquis inherited £1 million and, two years later, a further £4 million. Surprisingly, for a man who was to go down in the annals of the British aristocracy as a consummate profligate, he proved a very successful businessman and actually managed to increase his fortune with shrewd investment. But he also started spending it, extremely unshrewdly.

In 1983, he was charged in New York with heroin trafficking, the first of many such indictments. In 1985, he inherited the entire estate when his father died. This he proceeded to fritter away on drugs, cars, drink and sex – in 1988 it was reported that he had offered a male stripper $6000 to have sex with him but had promptly passed out before the contract could be fulfilled. When the Marquis died, it was estimated that he had spent £7 million on drugs over the course of his life. As one newspaper put it, a little smugly, he *"threw it away – together with his health and dignity."*

One of the more colourful heroin scandals to emerge in the 1990s occurred during the general election campaign of 1997 in the UK. A writer, travelling with the notoriously conventional then Prime Minister, John Major, on his campaign aeroplane, was found to be taking illicit substances in the lavatory. The writer in question was the *enfant terrible* of British literature and former heroin addict, Will Self. *"We can confirm we were recently made aware of reports of an alleged use of a controlled drug. At this stage we're not prepared to discuss details,"* stated the British police. Though Self at first denied the allegations, his newspaper, the *Observer* promptly sacked him. Later, in interviews with other papers, he admitted that he had taken drugs on the aeroplane.

Press and public alike love drug scandals. They represent "what should be": people get their comeuppance, pride is seen to take a fall and morality reclaims its rightful place. But there is another element to the satisfaction people derive from seeing stars and aristocrats humiliated and it is entirely ignoble. Part of us envies the person rich enough, or devil-may-care enough, to embark on a life of wanton self destruction but our jealousy is offset by witnessing their downfall. We judge the heroin addict not as a sick person but someone who has wilfully chosen a life contrary to the norms and expectations of society and small wonder if it all goes pear-shaped. The media love to publish morality tales and the public love to read them. But behind it all lies a comfortable and ultimately false feeling of self-righteousness.

THE MODERN AGE

DEFEAT FOR LIBERALISM

During the 1950s there was a last-ditch struggle by the forces of liberalism against the United States' drug laws. Articles in the more broad-minded newspapers began to question the appropriateness of such severe measures. At the centre of the debate was the question of whether it was appropriate, or even fruitful, to criminalize addicts and lock them up, or whether it was better to switch to a system whereby the addict was treated, with heroin. This was the system used in the UK and at that time it seemed to be working.

In 1954, the American Bar Association created a special committee on narcotics and, in 1955, called on Congress to re-examine the Harrison Act and make a full review of the federal enforcement policies developed under it. It is unlikely that the impetus behind this proposal was engendered by a new sense of liberalism in the ABA, more probably they were simply fed up with the increasing omnipotence of Anslinger and his band of merry men in this area. Nonetheless, it reflected a general recognition that perhaps the Anslinger way was not the only way.

By a strange coincidence, at the same time, Senator Price Daniel of Texas introduced a bill to authorize the senate judiciary committee *"to conduct a full and complete study of the narcotics problem in the United States, including ways and means of improving the Federal Criminal Code and other laws and enforcement procedures dealing with possession, sale, and transportation of narcotics, marijuana and similar drugs."* For "improving" read "tightening up". It soon became clear that Daniel was about as interested in any substantive change to the laws as Anslinger.

A race was on: on one side was the Senator, firmly in the Anslinger camp, on the other the ABA, now in association with the American Medical

US AGENTS SWIM, AS EVER, AGAINST THE TIDE

Association, who were similarly fed up with being dictated to by Anslinger's bunch of roughnecks. Unfortunately, the ABA/AMA's report, stymied by an inability to get funding, didn't get going until late 1956 and interim findings were not delivered until November 1957. The Daniel subcommittee, in contrast, started up post-haste. It was always going to be a one-sided affair, with the advocates of reform allowed only one-and-a half days to state their case, as opposed to ten months devoted to interviewing FBN supporters.

Much of the Daniel report was concerned with the idea of treating addicts as opposed to throwing them in jail. One of those called before it was Dr Hubert Howe, a proponent of clinic-based maintenance for drug addicts. At the hearing, he made these seemingly reasonable points:

"Many people recoil with horror at the suggestion of furnishing low-cost drugs to addicts, even under the best system of supervision which our Government can devise. For those of us who want to pass laws prohibiting everything undesirable, and many Americans seem to, it is a thoroughly startling idea. The public has yet to grasp the fact that addicts are dangerous when they are without their drugs, not when they are with them. They do not realize that in Britain this problem has been solved. The question, therefore, clearly is: Why should we have narcotic laws, the practical effect of which is to force people to rob, steal, proselytise, and prostitute, in order to support their habit, especially when the need for criminal activity can be prevented for a few cents' worth of drugs per addict, per day?

"One may also consider that, after 40 years of the Harrison Act, the addict still obtains his drug, unless he is in the strictest form of incarceration. We are not saying to give the addicts more drugs. We are simply advising a different method of distribution. The Government says he cannot get it legally; therefore, he has got to steal and rob, and so on, in order to get it. Well, he gets it, but we believe there is a better method of distribution than that. We are not in any way advocating that they get more than they need. But every addict gets his drug right now. As I say, unless he is in jail, every addict gets his drug and many of them get it in jail, at least they do in New York. Why not let him have his minimum requirement under licensed medical supervision, rather than force him to get it by criminal activities, through criminal channels? We now have, in the narcotic black market, a matchless machine for the manufacture of criminals. Isn't it about time we looked over the horizon to see how the problem has been solved elsewhere?"

Such views, however mildly put, were anathema to Senator Daniel's ears. One of the mainstays of American drug legislation was, and is, the assumption that addicts create addicts in the way that a vampire creates more vampires. From the early days, when anti-drug campaigners talked of " infection by the Chinese" this has been a constant theme in the drug war. It provides the rationale for excluding the addict from society, rather than letting him operate freely and socialize with friends, family and work colleagues. Another of the politicians at the hearing, Senator Butler, presented this article of faith to Doctor Howe as an argument against any sort of maintenance system:

"There has been some evidence here that some people become addicts simply to keep the addict comfortable or keep him company, or just to get in the swim, so to speak. Now, if it becomes generally known that addiction would be aided, and anybody who becomes an addict can always be kept in the happy and comfortable position of being satisfied, wouldn't you have a great tendency on the part of the addict to induce others to come in by simply saying, 'Well, here it is a wonderful thing and a wonderful sensation, and there is no harm, you don't take any chances now. You can come in and keep this going, and live in this beautiful state all your life at public expense.' Doesn't that multiply your addicts?"

Dr Howe's legitimate response to this, namely that if the addict was only given his drug in a hospital or clinic and not allowed to leave the premises with it, he would be unable to furnish his intended victim with a "taster", was brushed aside. Indeed, Senator Daniel, taking things one step further, had this idea: *"What would be wrong with a new set of laws that would follow your suggestion on not branding them as criminals, if that is all that they have ever done, but getting them in some kind of an institution or farm or something where they cannot spread their addiction to other people, and where you can try to do all these things about treating them and rehabilitating them?"*

Senator Daniel wrapped up the hearings with a reiteration of the "leper colony" principle:

"Gentlemen, I tell you that, after sitting through two more days of hearings here, I am convinced that we are never going to lick this problem of the drug traffic until we get the addicts off the streets of this country. They have got to be taken off the streets, and I know it is hard. Some of the enforcement officers think it is best to get them in the jails temporarily, and the different States have passed those kinds of laws. I would like to see us at the same time that we set up our laws to take them off the streets, set up some place to have them go and get a chance for treatment, and then if they won't take it, and you cannot do anything with them, then, it seems to me, it is just as humane to put them in some kind of a colony or some kind of farm or institution like you do mental patients." He finished off, one presumes rhetorically, with: *"Any other comments, gentlemen?"* Happily, his colony plan never materialized, although it was to resurface briefly with the advent of the AIDS epidemic in the 1980s.

The findings of Senator Daniel's committee were published in April 1956. Dr Howe and co need not have bothered – the report emanating from the committee found that the USA had the greatest number of addicts of any Western Country (true) and that these addicts were behind half the crime committed in metropolitan areas (questionable). It also reasserted the view that drug addiction was contagious and that addicts by nature attempted to convert others to their side. It recommended that addicts be isolated from society and that sentences for both possession and trafficking be raised. It also identified a new threat to the United States' war on heroin, namely Communist China's plot to flood the American market with the drug in an attempt to enfeeble the population in preparation for a communist take-over. This, despite the fact that Communist China is the only country this century to have successfully eradicated heroin use, albeit by decidedly despotic means.

The lion's share of the report was devoted to rubbishing the idea of any sort of maintenance programme, clinic-based or otherwise. It quoted one of their witnesses in defence of this position:

"One of the Nation's outstanding law-enforcement officers," the report said, *"Sheriff Owen W. Kilday, of Bexar County, Tex., testified that he, at one time, had strongly approved of the clinics as a possible means of destroying the drug peddler's market and, ultimately, the illicit narcotics traffic. However, due to an investigation in San Antonio which showed that a peddler had systematically enticed 40 to 50 boys and girls of high-school age to begin using narcotics, he came to the conclusion that 'If you did away with the market, they would create another one and I am opposed to it all the way. I don't believe there ought to be any clinic whatsoever'."*

With this, the report introduced another theme that has come to dominate the drug debate – that of innocent youth being corrupted by an older reprobate. It's a powerful image, one much in use in the late 1990s in the UK during a debate over the liberalization of the laws on homosexuality. The report even managed to fit in that narcotics made a man impotent and a woman sterile. Curiously, these were both seen as a misfortune for the man.

A NEW LAW

Senator Daniel's report bore fruit in the 1956 Narcotic Control Act, signed by President Dwight D. Eisenhower on July 18. This increased all sentences for all drug offences and introduced the death penalty for supplying heroin to a minor. Furthermore, there was to be no question of parole for anyone other than first-time offenders convicted of possession only. The potential for inhumanity in this last clause was swiftly realized: in 1957, a Mexican-American small-time crook, Gilbert Zaragoza, was arrested for selling heroin to a 17-year-old FBN plant, himself a former addict. Zaragoza was a 21-year-old epileptic with an IQ somewhere around seventy but nonetheless faced the full vigour of the newly empowered courts. He was duly sentenced to life (the jury couldn't quite stomach imposing the death penalty) which is what he got "to set an example to others" according to the presiding judge.

The 1956 Narcotic Control Act rather took the wind out of the sails of the ABA/AMA's report, of which an interim version was delivered in 1957. It reported, among other things, that a clinic be set up to treat drug addicts as an experiment. It also suggested that wholescale imprisonment was perhaps not the best solution to the United States' drug problem and that drug addicts should be treated primarily as sick people. It also questioned the model of the drug addict as "contagious".

Anslinger's response to these suggestions was characteristically contemptuous: *"For your kindness in sending me,"* he wrote, *"with your letter of February 24* [1958], *the interim report of the joint Committee of the American Bar Association and the American Medical Association on Narcotic Drugs and asking for comments and suggestions, I am grateful. As for my comment, after reading this report I find it incredible that so many glaring inaccuracies, manifest inconsistencies, apparent ambiguities, important omissions and even false statements could be found in one report on the narcotic problem."*

He continued, ever forthright, *"My suggestion is that the person (unquestionably prejudiced) who prepared this report should sit down with our people to make necessary corrections."* Elsewhere he wrote that *"the plan is so simple that only a simpleton could think it up. Certainly the ABA should have hired a lawyer to read the laws and find out what it is all about."*

In an issue of the FBI *Law Enforcement Bulletin*, Anslinger added the bizarre comment: *"Following the line of thinking of the 'clinic plan' advocates to a logical conclusion, there would be no objection to the state setting aside a building where on the first floor there would be a bar for alcoholics, on the second floor licensed prostitution, with the third floor set aside for sexual deviates and, crowning them all, on the top floor a drug-dispensing station for addicts."*

At times, Anslinger sounded insane, such was his determination not to give so much as an inch in his one-man fight against the sweeping tide of narcotics. *"The idea of establishing clinics for narcotic addicts where the addict can be furnished narcotics cheaply intrigues many people,"* he said again in response to the AMA/ABA report. *"Proponents of the idea naively assume that the person is quite normal as long as he can obtain narcotics. They should talk to doctor addicts who point out how their whole lives are meaningless except for one thing – and that is getting a shot four hours from now. Family, children, friends, and patients mean nothing to them. For example, in delivering a baby they will nonchalantly cut through into the rectum with no sense of remorse whatsoever, since in their state of mild euphoria nothing else is particularly important anyway."* Where he got this highly alarming fact from he never explained.

Needless to say, the ABA and AMA's efforts to bring some degree of humanity to the United States' drug laws were in vain, and Anslinger, as usual, carried the day. Soundly humiliated by Anslinger's well-organized campaign against them and their "lunatic, commie-inspired ideas", they retired from the fray to lick their wounds and have pretty much remained there ever since. As one judge, Chief Magistrate Murtagh, wrote: *"There is only one way to start reform. Retire Commissioner Anslinger and replace him with a distinguished public health administrator of vision and perception and, above all, heart."* Unfortunately he was not reckoning on Richard Nixon and Nelson Rockefeller.

A NEW WAR

By the end of the 1960s, the new President, Richard Nixon, found himself needing a cause. Discontent with the Vietnam War and growing questions about his probity were combining against him. Luckily, there was one ready and waiting on which most of the groundwork had already been done by the Governor of New York, Nelson Rockefeller. Rockefeller, ironically the great-grandson of a patent medicine peddler, had played the drug card to great success in his campaign for the governorship. In a 1966 rally he had said of his opponent: *"Frank O'Connor's election would mean narcotic addicts would continue to be free to roam the street – to mug, snatch purses, to steal, even to murder, or to spread the deadly infection that afflicts them possibly to your own son or daughter. Half the crime in New York City is committed by narcotic addicts."*

He followed up this alarming assertion with a challenge to the American people: *"Are the sons and daughters of a generation that survived a great depression and rebuilt a prosperous nation, that defeated Nazism and Fascism and preserved the free world, to be vanquished by a powder, needles, and pills?"* Of course they weren't, and Rockefeller was duly elected to the governorship.

Nixon, recognizing a good thing when he saw one, jumped on the band wagon. In the run-up to his 1972 re-election campaign, he made drugs one of his priorities and once elected, increasingly desperate to deflect interest away from the mysterious affair at the Watergate Hotel, declared "war on drugs". The first step taken in this war was to persuade Turkey to eradicate opium production. Nixon's statisticians announced that Turkey was ultimately responsible for 80 per cent of the heroin getting into the USA.

That this figure was entirely without foundation did nothing to stop it becoming a "fact". Turkey, under the influence of $35 million worth of US aid, set about persuading opium farmers to switch to other crops. How successful they were in this is open to question and, even if they were, it would have made little difference to world opium production, Nixon's 80 per cent statistic being a complete fiction. What was important to Nixon was that it was a public relations success – as Rockefeller pointed out, in 1973, *"Every poll of public concern documents that the number one growing concern of the American people is crime and drugs."*

After his "success" with Turkey, Nixon turned his attention to France. In an attempt to locate and destroy the heroin laboratories of Marseilles, which, unlike Turkey, probably did supply about 80 per cent of the United States heroin, American drug hounds employed a "heroin sniffer", a machine which could detect the acetic anhydrides used in manufacturing heroin. Concealed in a VW camper van with a snorkel mounted on its roof, the "sniffer" beetled round Marseilles seeking out the tell-tale fumes. Unfortunately, all it picked out was salad dressing and the drug squad reverted to more conventional methods. This meant getting the French police in on the deal. As noted before, the French police were prepared to leave the Corsicans alone so long as the heroin they were producing was going to America and not for domestic use. However, a new generation of drug barons was not prepared to dismiss a large potential market on their doorstep and had started diverting some heroin into France. So, with all deals off, the French police, quickly – some thought suspiciously so – rounded up a whole group of manufacturers and traffickers and shut down several labs.

However, while Nixon's advisers may have been correct in thinking that Marseilles was the route by which most heroin came to the USA, they were mistaken in thinking that its removal from the scene would encumber the traffickers. With Turkey out of the running, they went for supplies to south-east Asia which, thanks to the demand from American soldiers based there, was now producing class one heroin, nicknamed "China white". When Nixon realized this, he dispatched operatives to stem the flow from there as well. For once, it seemed that success was on the cards – the combination of the removal of Turkey from the scene, the crippling of the French Connection and the interruption of flow from south-east Asia produced a heroin drought in the USA of the sort not seen since the Second World War. Once again, US users turned to Mexico Meanwhile, the drug lords of south-east Asia had an abundance of heroin and no easy access to their market. The solution was simple – find another market. They found two: Western Europe and Australia

SINCE THE DISCONTINUATION OF THE "BRITISH SYSTEM" HEROIN IS UNLIKELY NOW TO BE FOUND IN SO PHARMACEUTICALLY PURE, AND HYGIENIC A STATE AS THIS.

THE "BRITISH SYSTEM"

Europe had not had much of a heroin problem up to this date. True, a new generation of Corsican traffickers had started to sell their wares closer to home but the numbers were still small. But in the UK the number of heroin addicts had been increasing – quite spectacularly – since 1960. Heroin addiction was seen as a disease in the UK and so had never been criminalized as it was in the USA. The basic guidelines for Britain's drug-abuse policy were established in 1926, a dozen years after America passed the Harrison Act, which set the US drugs policy. A committee chaired by Sir Humphrey Rolleston, a British doctor, said that doctors should be allowed to prescribe narcotics to wean patients off such drugs, to relieve pain after a prolonged cure had failed and in cases where small doses enabled otherwise helpless patients to perform "useful tasks" and lead relatively normal lives. The following passages from the Rolleston report demonstrate just how different the "British System" was to that of the USA.

"*Morphine or heroin may properly be administered to addicts in the following circumstances, namely, (a) where patients are under treatment by the gradual withdrawal method with a view to cure, (b) where it has been demonstrated, after a prolonged attempt at cure, that the use of the drug cannot be safely discontinued entirely, on account of the severity of the withdrawal symptoms produced, and (c) where it has been similarly demonstrated that the patient, while capable of leading a useful and relatively normal life when a certain minimum dose is regularly administered, becomes incapable of this when the drug is entirely discontinued."*

With respect to the handling of incurable addicts, the report directed:

"Precaution in Treatment of Apparently Incurable Cases. These will include both the cases in which the severity of withdrawal symptoms, observed on complete discontinuance after prolonged attempted cure, and the cases in which the inability of the patient to lead, without a minimum dose, a relatively normal life appear to indicate continuous administration of the drug indefinitely. They may be either cases of persons whom the practitioner has himself already treated with a view to cure, or cases of persons as to whom he is satisfied, by information received from those by whom they have been previously treated, that they must be regarded as incurable. In all such cases the main object must be to keep the supply of the drug within the limit of what is strictly necessary. The practitioner must, therefore, see the patient sufficiently often to maintain such observation of his condition as is necessary for justifying the treatment."

In the UK, heroin was yet to be linked with criminality – indeed most users before the 1960s tended to be middle class or from the medical profession. But, in 1958, the Minister of Health appointed a Review Committee to consider whether modifications should be made in the standards set forth by the 1926 Rolleston Report. The chairman was Sir Russell Brain, from whom the committee took its name. In November 1960, after extensive study and hearings, the Brain Committee made its report, concluding that no noteworthy difficulties had arisen from the policy of permitting doctors to provide drugs to known addicts, that the few irregularities which had come to light over the years did not warrant regulatory changes to correct them, that the problem of addiction was still "a small one," and that although there had been an increase in the use of cannabis it could not be classified as an addicting drug and required no special administrative measures as of that time. The Brain Committee's principal suggestion was that the Home Office Memorandum which contained the Rolleston Rules *"could be presented in a more readable form."*

But this first Brain Report came just when an influx of addicts from Canada and the USA was beginning to arrive in London, and soon thereafter the hippie movement started to grow in England, especially in London, where it seemed to have more vitality than parallel trends in the USA. Although not justifying the exultant cries raised by hard-line US narcotic authorities, there is no question that some new problems did appear to plague the British. Three or four London doctors, possibly as many as half a dozen, began to prescribe heroin in large amounts, defying the gentle sanctions that had theretofore sufficed to hold the medical profession in line. Marijuana smoking rose alarmingly. Abuse of amphetamines and barbiturates became more widespread, and the British press, doubtless once more reflecting somewhat the American excitement over the same subject, began giving these substances increased attention.

Addiction rates continued to rise and, in 1965, the Brain Committee was reconvened. A second report was issued that recommended the first significant restrictions on the prescribing of heroin in the UK. It was a shock to the British medical establishment that their system, a showpiece of enlightened and liberal drug policy, was now crumbling. Why was a system that had worked so well for forty years now failing to do the job? (This failure was much to the satisfaction of Henry Anslinger who, in 1961, wrote that the UK was responsible for 70 per cent of all heroin consumption. Where he got this wholly inaccurate figure from is unclear, but it is possible that he was including Hong Kong in his arithmetic.)

A LEGAL LOOPHOLE

Blame for the sudden worsening of the heroin problem was laid squarely at the feet of a large group of Canadian addicts who had started to arrive in the UK in the late 1950s and early 1960s. Canadian drug policy was broadly similar to United States policy so – hearing of Britain's more accommodating system and unencumbered, as members of the British Commonwealth, by immigration restrictions – hundreds of Canadian addicts landed in the UK, from 1958 onwards. That they were in the country for the drugs rather than the sights is borne out by this statement from one of them: "I got a taxi from the airport to a GP in the Holloway Road, [a street in the north of London] and got an immediate prescription for heroin and cocaine."

The Canadians revealed a basic fault in the "British System." It was open to abuse. For, while most British doctors acted with all probity, some perhaps lacked judgement. The Brain report recognized this dilemma:

"From the evidence before us we have been led to the conclusion that the major source of supply has been the activity of a very few doctors who have prescribed excessively for addicts. Thus we were informed that in 1962 one doctor alone prescribed almost 600,000 tablets

(6 million milligrams or 6 kilos) of heroin for addicts. The same doctor, on one occasion, prescribed 900 tablets (9,000 milligrams) of heroin to one addict and three days later prescribed for the same patient another 600 tablets (6,000 milligrams) 'to replace pills lost in an accident'."

The Brain report was loath to suggest that doctors were acting in anything other than good faith, but it is undeniable that some of them were only too well aware of their over-prescribing and some were more than happy to make a profit out of it. For instance one doctor, a dermatologist with a passion for gambling, funded his addiction by prescribing heroin by the cart load. He ended his professional days issuing prescriptions from a taxi parked in front of a tube station, where he was finally caught on a technicality. Another was reported to have issued prescriptions to 140 addicts with a daily average of six to eight grains at the height of his narcotics enterprise.

The Brain Commission wrestled with these dilemmas – they did not want to introduce a system such as that in the USA, where addiction was criminalized and thus could not be monitored or treated, but saw their own beloved system faltering.

"We have borne in mind the dilemma which faces the authorities responsible for the control of dangerous drugs in this country. If there is insufficient control it may lead to the spread of addiction as is happening at present. If, on the other hand, the restrictions are so severe as to prevent or seriously discourage the addict from obtaining any supplies from legitimate sources, [they] may lead to the development of an organized illicit traffic. The absence hitherto of such an organized illicit traffic has been attributed largely to the fact that an addict has been able to obtain supplies of drugs legally. But this facility has now been abused, with the result that addiction has increased."

The UK's way out of this quandary was to remove the right to prescribe heroin from general practitioners (GPs) and put it in the hands of clinics. In 1968, the compulsory notification of addicts went into effect, and the prescribing of heroin was restricted to doctors in the newly created treatment centres. But few addicts actually signed up. With heroin flooding in from the Far East there was no need to get your card permanently marked as an addict when you could get dope cheaply and readily on the street.

END OF STORY?

It did not, of course, take long for the Middle East's opium-producing regions to recover from Nixon's assault. Fuelled by political instability in the 1980s and 1990s, Afghanistan became the major producer in what is now known as "the Golden Crescent". Again it was America's fear of Communism outweighing its fear of drugs that spawned the regeneration of Afghanistan's poppy fields. When the Soviet Union invaded Afghanistan in 1979, the West was once again faced with the red peril in a geographically sensitive area.

Both the CIA and the UK's foreign intelligence service, MI6,

IN AFGHANISTAN A FARMER INSPECTS HIS UNHOLY CROP, PROVIDING FUNDS FOR A HOLY WAR

assisted the Mujahideen, the Afghan resistance, in their fight against the Russians. This they did mainly by supplying them with arms and training them up into an effective fighting force. In all, by the end of the war, the USA had funded the Mujahideen to the tune of $2 billion. The Mujahideen, when not fighting the Soviet invaders, controlled opium production in Afghanistan – a profitable sideline that funded their struggle. After the Soviet Army left in 1989, they abandoned a country awash with opium and in a state of total disarray.

Jack A. Blum, who from 1987–1989 served as the Special Counsel to the Senate Foreign Relations Committee, staffing the investigation by the Subcommittee on Narcotics, Terrorism, and International Operations, said this in a report to the Senate Select Committee on Intelligence on Drug Trafficking and the Contra War in October 1996:

"Our efforts in Afghanistan have helped turn the region into one of the world's largest producers and exporters of heroin. The war focused the Afghan farmers on their best crop – the opium poppy. The poppy requires little attention. Opium paste is lightweight, is very valuable, and can be moved to market over high mountains on the backs of donkeys. It is the perfect crop for people fighting a guerrilla war. That 'covert' operation has also produced a bumper crop of terrorists trained by us."

He might have added that Afghanistan quickly became embroiled in a civil war resulting in the dominance of the Taliban, perhaps the most oppressive and backward-looking regime in the world. The Taliban, unrecognized by the international community and thus ineligible for aid, see no reason to suppress their country's main export (though they have curiously banned the use of marijuana).

The Golden Triangle similarly has gone from strength to strength, with Myanmar producing more opium than anywhere else in the world. Even Mexico is now manufacturing higher grade heroin, providing yet another reliable source. Meanwhile, with the collapse of Communism in Europe at the end of the twentieth century, new markets have opened up, while chaos in the Balkans – the traditional smuggling route into Europe – has rendered policing of those areas almost impossible. It is hard to see heroin going quietly, if at all, when there is so much money to be made from it and so many places ready to supply it. As Myles Ambrose, one of Nixon's advisers in his war on drugs, later pointed out to his colleagues: *"The basic fact that eluded these great geniuses was that it takes only ten square miles of poppy to feed the entire American heroin market, and they grow everywhere."*

NEVER-ENDING STORY

ANCIENT HISTORY

This book has so far detailed the medical and legislative history of heroin. It has also dealt with the drug's cultural history. But to understand fully the unique place that heroin holds in international law and the public consciousness one must look at the history of opium. Heroin doesn't just owe its pharmacological essence to the juice of the opium poppy, *Papaver somniferum*. Heroin is the final chapter in the story of a plant that has been making waves for over a thousand years.

Opium's history is an ancient one. The Sumerians, who inhabited an area in what is now southern Iraq, from around 5000–2000BC, appear to have used it, suggested by the fact that they have an ideogram for it which has been translated as "hul", meaning joy or rejoicing. The name seems to imply that they were well aware of its properties. Several millennia later there is evidence of poppies being cultivated or used in Europe, through the fossil remains of poppy seeds found in Switzerland. Whether the poppies were being grown for their narcotic effect or for food (both uses continue to this day) we cannot tell. At the same time, opium use spread throughout the Mediterranean area and eastward through Asia, becoming an important commercial commodity. It appears that most was still being produced in the Middle East, while substantial amounts were being used in China, where it had probably been introduced by Arab traders.

It was Paracelsus (Theophrastus Philipus Aureolus Bombastus von Hohenheim, 1493–1541), believed by some to be the father of modern medicine, who first acknowledged the therapeutic properties of opium, at least as far as the West is concerned. He introduced it to the pharmacopoeia in the form of laudanum – opium dissolved in alcohol –

THE CHINESE WERE THE VICTIMS OF THE BIGGEST DRUG DEALER THE WORLD HAS EVER KNOWN - THE BRITISH EMPIRE

and, by 1680, the great English chemist Thomas Sydenham was able to say: *"Among the remedies which it has pleased the Almighty God to give to man to relieve his sufferings, none is so universal and efficacious as opium."* Others agreed – before long there were any number of preparations doing the rounds containing opium and claiming all sorts of properties. The most famous one was Dover's powder, created by the British doctor Thomas Dover, for the treatment of gout. It became the most widely used opium preparation for the next 150 years.

DRUG OF RECREATION

But while opium was increasingly being used for medicinal purposes in Europe (a job for which it is admirably suited), its recreational use was growing in China. This was abetted by Europe's recent discovery from the Americas, tobacco. Combining opium with tobacco made it much easier to smoke and European traders were quick to flood a huge market with not one but two products over which they had complete control. Despite resistance by the Chinese rulers (for instance in 1792 when the Emperor announced that anyone found keeping opium would be subject to death by strangulation) this situation prevailed until the beginning of the twentieth century.

There can be few plants over which two wars have been fought, but opium is one such. In 1838, the Emperor launched a moralistic anti-opium campaign that threatened Britain's nice little money spinner, and London dispatched a fleet of six warships, capturing Canton in May 1839. This marked the start of the First Opium War, which ended in 1842 with the Treaty of Nanking. This treaty required China to cede Hong Kong and open five new ports to foreign trade. But China still obstinately refused to legalize opium. So in 1856 the British, along with the French, again declared war. Again they won, captured the capital city, forced the Emperor to take to his heels, and burned the Imperial Summer Palace. In negotiations over the tariff provisions of the treaty that ended the Second Opium War, the British emissary, Lord Elgin, forced the Chinese to legalize opium imports.

Though opium use continued in Europe, its addictive qualities had been noted. More importantly, addiction became a problem. This seems obvious to us now, in a world where everyone is very familiar with the concept of addiction, but it wasn't always so. However, by the nineteenth century, books including Thomas de Quincey's *Confessions of an English Opium-eater*, published in 1822, make it clear that addiction, or at any rate opium addiction, was being seen as a vice. In 1806, morphine was isolated by the German chemist, Friedrich Sertürner. Sertürner named his discovery morphine, from Morpheus, the Roman god of sleep, and tested it on himself. His results were not encouraging: *"I consider it my duty,"* he wrote, *"to attract attention to the terrible effects of this new substance in order that calamity may be averted."*

His findings were entirely ignored by an eager public and medical profession, however, and morphine was immediately hailed as a non-addictive and more powerful substitute for opium. It was lauded as "God's own medicine" for its reliability, long-lasting effects and safety. When an Edinburgh doctor, Alexander Wood, invented the hypodermic syringe in 1850, morphine really took off, providing almost immediate pain relief. Dr Wood's wife achieved a notable first – as the first recorded person to die of hypodermic-induced overdose.

Throughout the nineteenth century, morphine addiction grew in the West, assisted by the easy availability of patent medicines laced with the stuff and by the American Civil War, which has been credited with creating an entire generation of young, male addicts. In the East, opium addiction ballooned, facilitated mainly by the efforts of the British East India company, who by now had a monopoly on the opium trade there and were making a fortune out of supplying China.

So many of heroin's characteristics throughout the twentieth century were already present in opium. It too was an international commodity of great value, though a legal one. Opium shared heroin's dubious status, hovering between medicinal and decadent. The other thing it shared in common with opium throughout history is that, while many civilizations have been well aware of its therapeutic and agreeable properties, none had understood why. None, that is, until the 1970s.

PLEASURE PRINCIPLE

In 1972, scientists at the Johns Hopkins university in the USA finally discovered what it was about opiates that was behind their well-established properties. They found that the human brain had "receptor sites" that were tailor-made for opiate drugs. A receptor site is a protein on the surface of a cell that allows only one type of chemical to bind with it in order to trigger a reaction by the cell. It seemed odd that the brain would have such sites, suggesting that the human race should, in fact, be taking heroin on a regular basis, until it was found that opiates had a very similar chemical structure to endorphins, a group of pain-relieving chemicals that occur naturally in the body ("endorphins" is short for "endogenous morphines"). They were not opiate receptors at all but endorphin receptors. But the name stuck. Taking heroin, which changes into morphine in the blood, stimulates these receptors, which send out the sort of chemicals usually reserved for relieving the pain of labour, injury or physical exertion.

Opiates provide a way of inducing an involuntary bodily reaction. While the body, rather meanly, will only allow you endorphins when you need them, opiates will march in and provide them on demand. It is pain relief without first having the pain. One can see, in theory, the attraction. But it doesn't go all the way to explaining heroin's extraordinary domination of the illicit drug trade and its cultural significance. Nor does it entirely explain why some people become addicted to the drug, while others display no interest in it.

PROFIT PRINCIPLE

In 1995, Joseph D. McNamara, a former chief of police in the USA, wrote an article for the National Review on the drug debate with the opening words:

"It's the money, stupid. After 35 years as a police officer in three of the country's largest cities, that is my message to the righteous politicians who obstinately proclaim that a war on drugs will lead to a drug-free America. About $500 worth of heroin or cocaine in a *source country will bring in as much as $100,000 on the streets of an American city. All the cops, armies, prisons, and executions in the world cannot impede a market with that kind of tax-free profit margin. It is the illegality that permits the obscene mark-up, enriching drug traffickers, distributors, dealers, crooked cops, lawyers, judges, politicians, bankers, businessmen."*

If you were an impoverished farmer and had to choose between growing rice, with almost no profit margin, and opium, with enough of a profit to buy the rice you need and still have some money left over, what would you grow? These are, after all, the principles on which Western capitalism has flourished – we can hardly be aggrieved at the Hunan hill farmer's adoption of them. Opium provides substantial rewards for its producers, though these are nothing to the financial payoff it brings to the next man up the line. For, along every step of opium/heroin production, there is another mark-up – by the time heroin reaches the streets its price has so magnified that the amount a consumer is paying for his one wrap is probably no less than the farmer got paid for his entire field of opium poppies. Everyone else along the way has got rich – in fact the only

PAPAVER SOMNIFERUM IN FULL BLOOM, JUST BEFORE IT IS MILKED FOR ITS NARCOTIC JUICES

people who generally get burnt in the heroin production/supply line are the two at either end, the farmer and the user.

About three months after the poppy seeds are planted, brightly coloured flowers bloom at the tips of greenish, tubular stems. As the petals fall away, they expose an egg-shaped seed pod. Inside the pod is an opaque, milky sap. This is opium in its crudest form. The sap is extracted by slitting the pod vertically in parallel strokes with a special curved knife. As the sap oozes out, it turns darker and thicker, forming a brownish-black gum. A farmer collects the gum with a scraping knife, bundles it into bricks, cakes or balls and wraps them in a simple material such as plastic or leaves. This is sometimes eaten, or smoked, locally. But no one gets rich that way. The real money is in export. It is at this point that opium enters the black market.

A merchant or broker buys the packages for transport to a morphine refinery. Very possibly he does his own refining, otherwise he will sell the blocks on to a refiner, most likely nearby. This obviates the need to transport opium, which is bulky and odorous, large distances with the attendant risks of detection. At the refinery, which may be little more than a rickety laboratory equipped with oil drums and shrouded in a jungle thicket, the opium is mixed with lime in boiling water. A precipitate of organic waste sinks to the bottom. On the surface, a white band of morphine forms. This is drawn off, reheated with ammonia, filtered and boiled again until it is reduced to a brown paste. The morphine thus produced is about one tenth the volume of the opium used to produce it, although just as potent. Here, the original refiner may sell it on to a heroin refiner, in which case he will put a considerable financial mark-up on it. Alternatively, he will have the know-how to do it himself, thus boosting his profits still further.

In his book *Opium – A History*, Martin Booth writes: *"First, equal quantities of morphine and acetic anhydride are heated in a glass or enamel-lined container for six hours at 85°C. The morphine and the acid combine to form impure diacetylmorphine. Second, water and chloroform are added to the solution to precipitate impurities. The solution is drained and sodium carbonate added to make the heroin solidify and sink. Third, the heroin is filtered out of the sodium carbonate solution with activated charcoal and purified with alcohol.* [Fourth,] *this solution is gently heated to evaporate the alcohol and leave heroin, which may be purified further..."*

If it does not receive this further purification, the substance is called "number three heroin", otherwise known as "mud" or "brown sugar" because of its brown colour. It is this type that was being produced in Mexico until recently and in South-east Asia until the arrival of American GIs there. Until the Americans appeared, the

A MERCHANT UNWRAPS HIS PRECIOUS CARGO OF CRUDE OPIUM PASTE

Europeans had managed to keep mastery of the final, and delicate step in heroin purification, to themselves. *"In the hands of a careless chemist the volatile ether gas may ignite and produce a violent explosion that can level a clandestine laboratory,"* writes Booth. The final refined product is a fluffy, white powder that is known in the trade as "number four heroin" and on the street as "white lady", "white boy", "white girl", "white nurse", etc.

From here, the heroin goes to the big brokers who organize the traffic from the supply points to the points of consumption. They usually deal in bulk shipments of 20–100kg (44–220lb). A broker in New York or Europe might divide a bulk shipment into wholesale lots of 1–10kg (2–22lb) for sale to underlings. The one-kilo bricks are often brightly packaged and imprinted with brand names worthy of beer or chocolate manufacturers. Heroin originating in Myanmar's Shan State, for example, sports a red-lettered logo, "Double UO Globe Brand", framed by a pair of lions. Even heroin dealers are not averse to the notion of brand identity, it seems.

Not many years ago, virtually all the heroin sold on the streets of the USA was so heavily diluted that it was rarely more than 10 per cent pure. Purity improved rapidly in the mid 1990s – routinely reaching 50–60 per cent – as dealers tried to expand their market beyond those addicts who inject heroin into their veins with hypodermic needles. Higher purity means heroin can be inhaled or smoked. This lack of needles makes heroin less alarming to the newcomer, especially since the advent of AIDS in the 1980s. By the time heroin is peddled on city streets in small bags its value has ballooned more than ten-fold since its arrival from Afghanistan or Myanmar/Burma. It is an estimate, but heroin probably multiplies its value by ten at every stage of the production and delivery process.

The profit margins involved in the heroin trade are clearly enormous. What then of overall figures? These are notoriously hard to estimate – for that is what they must always be in a business where no one fills in tax returns or customs forms. The last United Nations estimate of heroin production, for the 1990s, was approximately 300 tons, estimated largely by extrapolation from seizures – a notoriously inaccurate method. It is impossible to say how much this quantity is worth – where and to whom? From the perspective of the street consumer in Western Europe, it is clearly worth rather more than to the bulk buyer in Saigon.

AFGHAN PROBLEM

That the problem of heroin is inseparable from its economics is demonstrated by the situation in Afghanistan. It has already been noted that opium production in Afghanistan increased during the war with the Soviet Union. The Taliban, by the end of the 1990s the dominant force in Afghanistan, financed its holy war with profits from the world's second-largest opium crop. Nearly three-quarters of the heroin reaching Western Europe originates in Afghanistan, and most of this is grown in areas the Taliban controls. Recent satellite surveys show that opium production has soared in these regions.

In 1996, senior United Nations officials met the new rulers of Kabul to discuss aid to the devastated country. But the Taliban's apparent unwillingness to curb opium production proved a stumbling block in negotiations. The Taliban claimed that the opium plantations were in territories outside their control. This is hardly likely – there is little left of Afghanistan beyond Taliban control. *"They can't continue to receive all sorts of assistance – food, clothing and medical – from major donors and export this poison to the same countries that are helping them,"* said Giovanni Quaglia, regional director of the UN control programme at the time. But on the other side, a representative of Afghanistan's struggle against drug production, Shamsul Haq Sayeed, claimed: *"The United States put pressure on us, but they didn't help the farmers. Our people are very poor in the era of war. But the US is not helping to stop cultivation. They're only talking."*

The problem has reached an impasse. No international aid will be forthcoming to Afghanistan until attempts are made to curtail opium production (the traditional leverage employed by the West in these matters). But with an opium harvest worth about £30 million a year to the farmers, it seems unlikely that the Afghans are going to do as they are told. *"We let people cultivate poppies,"* said Abdul Rashid, the head of the Taliban's drug control unit, in 1997, *"because farmers get good prices. We cannot push the people to grow wheat, there would be an uprising against the Taliban if we forced them to stop poppy cultivation."* Nor are the Taliban necessarily any keener to curtail opium cultivation. The Taliban's war was waged on the proceeds from poppies and most likely that has remained its main source of income ever since. If the farmers are getting $30 million a year, who knows what their immediate superiors in the heroin chain are getting or – most importantly – who they are?

Camel or donkey trains first carry the harvest to heroin laboratories hidden in the Khyber Pass, on the border between Afghanistan and Pakistan. From there, the drug is smuggled through what used to be Soviet Central Asia to Europe and the USA. In 1996, Pakistani troops, acting under pressure from America, destroyed some laboratories in the Khyber Pass. But the primitive labs, mere shacks containing a few steel drums, were simply moved.

International drug control agencies have been unwilling to get embroiled in the chaos of Afghanistan. The UN Drug Control Programme office in Kabul has not been staffed for four years, and UN involvement in a control scheme in the Afghan city of Jalalabad (near the Khyber Pass) has been wound up.

Mullah Omar Akhund, the Taliban leader, declared in 1996 that the movement was anti-heroin, anti-hashish and anti-drugs. But while it seems to have held true to the second of these declarations, the first looks like so much window dressing. Most western observers believe these pronouncements – and public, televised displays of Puritanism, such as smashing consignments of alcohol with a tank – are largely rhetoric.

The impasse in Afghanistan represents a real problem. Conditions in the country are desperate and they are in urgent need of aid. But the aid will not be forthcoming so long as the country's leaders continue to accept, perhaps encourage, opium cultivation. It is affirmation of just how much the poppy is worth to people and what they are prepared to sacrifice for it. The situation in Afghanistan should also be a salient reminder to the Western democracies who effectively produced this state of affairs through their anti-Soviet machinations. You can't have it both ways.

So much for heroin as a money spinner. It clearly mitigates hugely against any quick solutions being found in the war on drugs when so much is at stake – the fate of an entire country, for instance. But having explained why people are prepared to be involved in the heroin trade, one is left with the *raison d'être* for that trade – the consumer. Why do people take heroin?

COLD TURKEY

From a purely physiological point of view, the attraction of heroin is easy enough to explain. Because opiates are doing what the body is meant to do by itself, by locking on to the opiate receptors, they give pleasure. Continued use of opiates leads to addiction, making the body reliant on the presence of the drug for pleasure. The brain's natural chemistry is first usurped by morphine and then supplanted. Soon the body is unable to function normally without the "impostor endorphins", the real ones having long since packed their bags and called it a day.

Withdrawal of the drug leads to the classic "cold turkey", symptoms of tremors, nausea, cramps, muscle spasms, fever and so on, as the body is no longer able to cope without its artificial sustenance. We all know about these symptoms from their regular depiction in film and television – think of *Christian F*, the 1981 film about a young German girl hooked on drugs. All the usual indicators of withdrawal are there – she's tied to her bed, locked in her room, going through hideous agonies and would sell her soul for another fix. It's an appealingly simple model for addiction, but also a rather misleading one. It seems satisfyingly moral – it conforms to the general supposition that one should not interfere with what nature intended. Who, after all, are we to go around playing God with our brain chemicals? But it also makes addiction appear to be an entirely physiological state, when all the evidence would seem to suggest that addiction has, at the very least, a strong psychological component.

In 1964, the World Health Organization wrote in a report: *"Physical dependence is an inevitable result of the pharmacological action of some drugs with sufficient amount and time of administration. Psychic dependence, while also related to pharmacological action, is more particularly a manifestation of the individual's reaction to the effects of a specific drug and varies with the individual as well as the drug."* At the time, opiate receptors had yet to be discovered so all anyone had to go on was the observation of addicts, from which they derived a fairly obvious conclusion. But since the discovery of the opiate receptors, king science has ruled the roost and "psychic dependence" has gone out the window, along with any hope of treating it.

INDIAN GOUACHE FROM 1870 DEPICTING THE SELLING AND SMOKING OF OPIUM

The other problem with the physiological addiction model is that it makes both addiction and consequently agonizing withdrawal a necessary adjunct of opiate use. At the risk of destroying a thousand government health campaigns, this is not the case. It takes a while to become an opiate addict. Thomas de Quincey reckoned that: *"Making allowance for constitutional differences, I should say that in less than 120 days, no habit of opium-eating could be formed strong enough to call for any extraordinary self-conquest in renouncing it, even suddenly renouncing it. On Saturday you are an opium eater, on Sunday no longer such."*

Heroin is probably more addictive but nonetheless it usually takes considerably more than one "hit" to get hooked, contrary to popular belief and the rather useful line peddled by the *"Just Say No"* brigade. In addition to any pleasant effects opiates might have they also induce a general reduction in respiratory and cardiovascular activity, a depression of the cough reflex, itching, dilation of the pupils, constipation, and nausea and vomiting (remember the dogs). Most people, unsurprisingly, do not enjoy their first experience with heroin. It takes time to work up significant tolerance to heroin, and no little determination.

It is also, controversially, not the case that all people who take heroin on some sort of regular basis are what are generally considered addicts. A 1974 study of GIs returning from Vietnam who had regularly used heroin there found that not only were they able to stop using the drug upon their return , but also to continue to use it on occasion without falling into a cycle of addiction. *"Contrary to conventional belief,"* the report noted, *"the occasional use of narcotics without becoming addicted appears possible even for men who have previously been dependent on narcotics."*

All this leaves the question of why and how some people do become addicted to heroin, in the sense that we understand it: needing the drug just to get by. There's no easy answer, and as long as we insist on the rather simplistic model of physical addiction, not one anyone is likely to find. But if we are ever going to understand heroin addiction – surely a precondition of treating it – it is an answer that must be found.

DRUG USERS ARE PEOPLE TOO

This book has touched upon some of the groups of people who have used heroin since its synthesis. They have all been "celebrities". This is largely because these are the people whose use is most recorded. It needs to be remembered that the vast majority of addicts are people you have never heard of, living unremarkable lives little different from anyone else's, other than in their addiction. Nonetheless, describing the different cultures that have adopted heroin over the years does serve a purpose, for each of them reveals a possible reason for the addict's attraction to the drug. For instance, with many jazz musicians the appeal seemed to lie in the ability of the drug to provide a shelter against the iniquities of life as a black performer in the earlier half of the twentieth century. For the rock industry, heroin was the ultimate nihilism, the trip from which there was no return.

It has to be remembered that famous addicts are still addicts, and whatever propelled them into addiction could just as easily propel anyone into addiction. Thus, take away the jazz and you have the alienation that any black man or woman of that generation might feel. Remove the Fender guitars and Woodstock and perhaps all you have is a dissatisfied generation, cheated by their leaders and devoid of hope.

Perhaps it is stretching the point, but it does seem that the cultural movements most identified with heroin use – jazz, rock, beat and grunge – have all been movements of protest and dissatisfaction of one sort or another. It would fit heroin's iconic status as the ultimate no-go area. If this were true, one has to ask whether raising heroin to such an iconic status is such a good idea.

It would be ironic to find that the machinations of the great anti-drug propagandists of the twentieth century, from Captain Hobson to Nancy Reagan, had only succeeded in creating a world population of rebellious teenagers eager to do as they weren't told to. It's a simplistic analysis, but no more so than most of the stuff coming out of government health warnings.

Unfortunately, not enough research is being done in this area. Heroin addiction remains the object of simplistic analysis, centring on physical addiction. It is easier that way: heroin is evil and you shouldn't go near it. It is highly addictive and will turn you into a criminal or prostitute within minutes. It will either kill you or turn your life into a zombie misery. End of story. There is something of the ostrich burying his head in the sand about all this. While we refuse to properly engage with what heroin really means to those who take it and why they continue to do so, heroin is not going to go away, however much money is thrown at the war on drugs, however many powers are given to the police.

The assumption that heroin itself rather than any other factors is the sole cause of addiction underpins contemporary treatment methods for addiction. Treatment relies exclusively on removing this *sole* cause of the addiction. This is the theory underpinning methadone maintenance, the blue riband method of heroin treatment.

METHADONE MAINTENANCE

Methadone hydrochloride is an opioid (a synthetic opiate) that was originally synthesized by the German pharmaceutical company Axis during the Second World War. It was first marketed as "Dolophine" (in honour of Adolph Hitler) and was used as an analgesic for the treatment of severe pain. Its part in the treatment of heroin addiction dates from the 1950s, when it was used in reduction programmes in correctional institutions. First, heroin was replaced with methadone and then the amount of methadone being dispensed was gradually reduced until it could be dispensed with. It is an old idea and sounds all right in principle.

In various forms, the idea of use reduction has existed since people first started becoming concerned about addiction in the nineteenth century. A royal decree given by the second King of Thailand in 1809 suggested a course of self-treatment for opium dependence consisting of gradually cutting down the daily dosage until complete abstinence was reached. William Burroughs also tried a variation on this, which he describes in *Junky*. He bought a bottle of morphine and when it was half finished he topped it up with water. He continued with this diluted form again until half way through, at which point he once more topped it up with water. The theory was that after a while he'd be taking pure water and would have weaned himself off the junk. Of course he didn't and in a matter of days was off trying to score some more.

In 1967, two doctors, Vincent Dole and Marie Nyswander, started using methadone in a different way. They had joined forces to study the way heroin is metabolized in the human body. Dole came to this through his studies of obesity, where he had concluded that a tendency to overeat was not a question of greed, but a metabolic abnormality. He reasoned that heroin addiction might run along similar lines. Knowing nothing about narcotic addiction, he contacted Dr Nyswander, a psychiatrist who specialized in the treatment of drug addicts. She had long come to the conclusion that current methods of addiction treatment in the USA – suspension of access to the drug – were not working.

Dole and Nyswander joined forces and started their research. Their project at this stage was simply to examine the metabolisms of opiate addicts, with a view to further understanding the mechanics of addiction. They consequently enlisted two volunteers, both long-term heroin addicts, and filled them up with copious quantities of morphine, regularly, while Dr Dole put them through various metabolic tests. The patients were happy. Dr Dole commented: *"Much of the time they sat passively, in bathrobes, in front of a television set. They didn't respond to any of the other activities offered them. They just sat there, waiting for the next shot."*

Once the metabolic tests were completed, Dole and Nyswander were faced with the unenviable task of getting their volunteers off heroin – the law demanded it. So, as was usual, they substituted methadone for the morphine with a view to reducing the methadone bit by bit and hoping for a miracle. But, in order to complete their metabolic tests, they kept the patients on a high dose of methadone for longer than was customary. They were astonished by what happened. Instead of lounging around in their bath robes as before, they were all of a sudden galvanized into useful activity. *"The older addict began to paint industriously and his paintings were good,"* Dr Nyswander later told Nat Hentoff of the *New Yorker*. *"The younger started urging us to let him get his high school-equivalency diploma. We sent them both off to school, outside the hospital grounds, and they continued to live at the hospital."*

It appeared that Dole and Nyswander had inadvertently discovered a way of satisfying an addict's craving for drugs while allowing him or her to remain in society. The solution was methadone maintenance, it seemed, rather than methadone-based reduction. Methadone maintenance, which took off almost immediately, means methadone for life – there is no longer any imperative to get the addict off all drugs, just on to a different one. The slight absurdity of this position is brushed aside by the incontestable assumption that anything has got to be better than heroin. But this assumption has more to do with irrational prejudice than with impartial science.

Dole reported of their early volunteers: *"The interesting thing about methadone treatment is that it permits people to become whatever they potentially are. Whereas addicts, under the pressure of drug abuse and drug-seeking look very much the same, when they are freed from this slavery they differentiate and become part of the spectrum of humanity."*

This is the classic stereotype of the heroin addict: anti-social, interested only in his next fix and incapable of any useful contribution to society. But it's not necessarily an accurate picture. Two examples suffice to demonstrate this: in 1995, Dr Clive Froggatt, the British Government's health adviser, was sentenced to a 12-month jail sentence suspended for two years for obtaining heroin by deception. At his trial, he denied that his addiction had any impact on his work for the Government, which had involved whole-scale reforms of the health service. *"It did not really matter what I was addicted to, drugs or whatever, the point was I had a medical problem of being an addict."*

No-one saw fit to re-examine his reforms, confirming this opinion. In the USA, the leading surgeon and first professor of surgery at The Johns Hopkins Hospital, William Stewart Halsted, was a morphine addict for the last decades of his life. His secret was kept hidden carefully until the publication of Sir William Osler's private diary in 1969. Osler had been Halsted's physician while Osler was on the Hopkins faculty. Halsted's addiction did not appear to interfere with his work.

Drs Dole and Nyswander's results were greeted with delight and before long a clinic opened in Manhattan General Hospital devoted to methadone maintenance. No one seemed to make the obvious point that the patients were still addicts, just to a different drug.

METHADONE "GOOD" HEROIN "BAD"

Methadone maintenance does beg the question: if methadone, why not heroin? Is the latter so much more dangerous a drug than the former that its administration is to be preferred? Our immediate reaction is to say yes. But is this actually the case? If not, the rationale behind methadone maintenance goes out the window, not withstanding the fact that in most countries it remains illegal to prescribe heroin (this is not the case in the UK, where heroin prescription remains legal, although it is rarely prescribed today). If one rejects the rhetoric surrounding heroin, that it is somehow intrinsically bad, or Chinese, or communist, or crime-provoking or whatever, there seems little reason why one form of opiate addiction is any better than another. But very few either wish to or can make this leap of the imagination.

From the eighteenth century onwards, opium, morphine and heroin have all been associated with criminality. Not just by virtue of being illegal, but inherently. This was necessary to whip up the sort of public hysteria needed to justify what have often been disproportionately draconian legislation and sentencing and has been useful to a number of politicians in need of a cause, or a scapegoat. Sometimes it is society itself that needs the scapegoat – for the breakdown in family values, for the rising levels of crime, for just about anything. Heroin addicts fit the bill nicely and rarely get the chance to have their say on the matter, being likely to find themselves in prison if they do.

Every now and then, however, someone has spoken out to question this assumption, usually to be drowned out by such a chorus of disapproval or incredulity that you would think he had proposed the return of human sacrifice. One such was Dr Hubert Howe, who had testified to the Daniel subcommittee in 1955 on the subject of setting up maintenance clinics for heroin addicts. When asked whether allowing addicts to continue taking drugs would merely unleash a reign of terror on the streets, he pointed out that *"There is no definitive evidence that anything like that occurs as far as opiates go. Opiates are sedatives. If they take enough of them they put them to sleep."* And in response to the idea that heroin addicts were all of a kind – a criminal kind, best locked up for the good of society, he said this: *"But you must realize, that addicts are not a homogeneous group. They are everything from doctors and lawyers and ministers and everything else all the way down, and I do not think you could very well establish a Devil's Island and put them all there. What they need is to be gotten back into society, gotten back where they can hold down jobs."* As already explained, Dr Howe might as well have been talking to himself. Clinics were not for America.

SWITZERLAND'S HEROIN EXPERIMENT

One country that has tried a new approach to heroin addiction is Switzerland. In an article in the *New Republic*, Ethan Nadelmann, director of The Lindesmith Center, explained it this way: the Swiss Government is selling heroin to hard-core drug users. But in doing so, the Government isn't offhandedly facilitating drug abuse; it's conducting a national scientific experiment to determine whether prescribing heroin, morphine, and injectable methadone will save Switzerland both money and misery by reducing crime, disease and death.

The Swiss deal with drug users much as the USA and other countries do – by means of drug-free residential treatment programmes, oral methadone, prisons and so on – but they also know that these approaches are not enough. They first tried establishing a "Needle Park" in Zurich, an open drug scene where people could use drugs without being arrested. Most Zurichers, including the police, initially regarded the congregation of illicit drugs injectors in one place as preferable to scattering them throughout the city. But the scene grew unmanageable and city officials closed it down in February 1992. A second attempt faced similar problems and was shut down in March 1995.

So Needle Park wasn't the solution, but a heroin prescription programme might be. Here, 340 addicts receive a legal supply of heroin each day from one of the nine prescribing programmes in eight different cities. In addition, eleven receive morphine, and thirty-three receive injectable methadone. The programmes accept only "hard-core" junkies – people who have been injecting for years and who have attempted and failed to quit. Participants are not allowed to take the drug home with them. They have to inject on site and pay 15 francs (approximately $13) per day for their dose.

The idea of prescribing heroin to junkies in the hope of reducing their criminal activity and their risk of spreading AIDS and other diseases took off in 1991. Expert scientific and ethical advisory bodies were established to consider the range of issues. The International Narcotics Control Board – a United Nations organization that oversees international anti-drug treaties – had to be convinced that the Swiss innovation was an experiment, which is permitted under the treaty, rather than an official shift in policy. In Basel, opponents of the initiative demanded a city-wide referendum – in which 65 per cent of the electorate approved a local heroin prescription programme. The argument that swayed most people was remarkably straightforward: only a controlled scientific experiment could determine whether prescribing heroin to addicts is feasible and beneficial.

The experiment started in January 1994. The various programmes differ in some respects, although most provide supplemental doses of oral methadone, psychological counselling and other assistance. Some are located in cities such as Zurich, others in towns like Thun, at the foot of the Bernese Alps. Some provide just one drug, whereas others offer a choice. Some allow clients to vary their dose each day, others work with clients to establish a stable dosage level. One of the programmes in Zurich is primarily for women. The other Zurich programme permits addicts to take home heroin-injected cigarettes known as reefers, or "sugarettes" (heroin is called "sugar" by Swiss junkies).

It also conducted a parallel experiment in which twelve clients were prescribed cocaine reefers for up to twelve weeks. The results were mixed, with many of the participants finding the reefers unsatisfying. However, since more than two-thirds of Swiss junkies use cocaine as well as heroin, the Swiss hope to refine the cocaine experiment in the future.

The national experiment is designed to answer a host of questions that also bubble up in debates over drug policy in the USA, but that drug-war blinkers cause people to ignore. Can junkies stabilize their drug use if they are assured of a legal, safe, and stable source of heroin? Can they hold down a job even if they are injecting heroin two or three times a day? Do they stop using illegal heroin and cut back on the use of other illegal drugs? Do they commit fewer crimes? Are they healthier and less likely to contract the HIV virus? Are they less likely to overdose? Is it possible to overcome the "not in my back yard" objections that so often block methadone and other programmes for addicts. The answers to these questions are just beginning to come in. In late 1994, the Social Welfare Department in Zurich held a press conference to issue its preliminary findings:

- Heroin prescription is feasible, and has produced no black market in diverted heroin.
- The health of the addicts in the programme has clearly improved.
- Heroin prescription alone cannot solve the problems that led to the heroin addiction in the first place.
- Heroin prescription is less a medical programme than a social-psychological approach to a complex personal and social problem.
- Heroin per se causes very few, if any, problems when it is used in a controlled fashion and administered in hygienic conditions.

Programme administrators also found little support for the widespread belief that addicts' cravings for heroin are insatiable. When offered practically unlimited amounts of heroin (up to 300 milligrams three times a day), addicts soon realized that the maximum doses provided less of a "flash" than lower doses, and cut back their dosage levels accordingly.

On the basis of these initial findings, the Swiss Federal Government approved an expansion of the experiment – one that may offer an opportunity to address the bigger question that small-scale experiments and pilot projects cannot answer: Can the controlled prescription of heroin to addicts take the steam out of the illegal drug markets?

Switzerland's prescription experiment fits in with the two-track strategy that they and other Western European countries have been pursuing since the mid 1980s: tough police measures against drug dealers, and a "harm reduction" approach toward users. The idea behind harm reduction is to stop pretending that a drug-free society is a realistic goal; focus first on curtailing the spread of AIDS – a disease that cost the USA $15.2 billion by the end of 1995, and the lives of over 125,000 Americans – and later on curtailing drug use. The effort to make sterile syringes more readily available, through needle-exchange programmes and the sale of needles in pharmacies and vending machines, epitomizes the harm-reduction philosophy. Swiss physicians and pharmacists – along with their professional associations – are outspoken in their support for these initiatives. Study after study, including one conducted for the USA Centers for Disease Control, show that increasing needle availability reduces the spread of AIDS, gets dirty syringes off the streets, and saves money.

The Swiss have also created legal *Fixerräume*, or "injection rooms", where addicts can shoot up in a regulated, sanitary environment. Swiss public-health officials regard this harm-reduction innovation as preferable to the two most likely alternatives: open injection of illicit drugs in public places, which is distasteful and unsettling to most non-addicts; and the more discreet use of drugs in unsanctioned "shooting galleries" that are frequently dirty, violent, controlled by drug dealers, and conducive to needle sharing. Five *Fixerräume*, have now opened in Switzerland. Initial evaluations indicate that they are effective in reducing HIV transmission and the risk of overdose.

So what does the future hold? In 1999, Switzerland's governing body, the Federal Council, voted to expand the number of prescription slots to one thousand: eight hundred for heroin, one hundred each for morphine and injectable methadone. Interior Minister Ruth Dreifuss, who initially was sceptical of the experiment, is now a strong supporter. She is backed by the ministers of justice, defence and finance, who together constitute what has become known as "the drug delegation" of the Federal Council. The three leading political parties have combined to issue a joint report on drug policy that supports the heroin experiment and other harm-reduction initiatives.

Outside Switzerland, the Dutch are about to embark on their own modest experiment with heroin prescription. The Australians, who recently conducted an extensive feasibility study, seem likely to start a heroin-prescription programme. In Germany, officials in Frankfurt, Hamburg, Karlsruhe, Stuttgart and elsewhere are seeking permission from the central government to begin their own heroin-prescription projects.

While these countries experiment with more sensible and humane approaches to drug policy, the USA clings to a war not only against drug dealers, but also against drug users. Most scientific researchers studying drug abuse acknowledge that the Swiss experiment makes sense socially, economically and morally. The point of these innovations is not to coddle drug users. It is to reduce the human and economic costs of drug use – costs paid not only by users but also by non-users through increased health-care, justice and law-enforcement expenditures.

But no distinguished researcher seems prepared to take on all the forces blocking a heroin-prescription experiment in the USA. Through their reticence, they are shutting their eyes to drug policy options that could reduce crime, death, and disease and ultimately save the USA billions of dollars.

US INTRANSIGENCE

The American anti-maintenance bias can be explained, as can so much of their drug policy, by that country's early legislation. The USA did once have clinics, at the beginning of the twentieth century, but their existence was short-lived. The first was opened in 1912 by Charles Terry, the public health officer of Jacksonville, Florida, where he provided both opiates and cocaine. Others followed, particularly after the Treasury Department, in enforcement of the Harrison Act, prosecuted or threatened with prosecution health professionals who supplied addicts indefinitely. At this stage, the exact scope of the Harrison Act had not been determined and it was thought that prescribing heroin in a controlled, clinical environment might still be permissible. In New York State, registration of addicts was permitted so that physicians would restrict maintenance to those already addicted.

In New York City, the Health Department did not wish to provide opiates, morphine and heroin on an indefinite basis but did open a clinic at their city headquarters. This clinic provided heroin, but only as an inducement to registration and eventual detoxification and rehabilitation. About 7,500 addicts registered, received their drug of choice in dosages gradually decreased until uncomfortably small, usually three to eight grains of morphine daily, and were offered curative treatment. Most declined to be cured. Those who did receive treatment, at North Brother Island, seemed both unappreciative and very liable – the estimate was 95 percent – to return to narcotics available on the street or from a physician or druggist.

The Treasury Department, armed with fresh Supreme Court decisions about interpretation of the Harrison Act, in March 1919, started to close down the clinics, as well as prosecuting the dispensing physicians and druggists. The Treasury Department argued that the availability of easy maintenance was a disincentive to seeking a cure and that giving legal permission for maintenance clinics undermined the department's position when it brought action against a professional for reckless provision of drugs. From a legal point of view, the reckless provider was obeying the tax laws, as was the clinic, unless the Federal Government wanted to get into the question of medical competence, which was a state, not a federal, concern.

Gradually the clinics were closed, the last one in 1925 in Knoxville, Tennessee. Some had been operated poorly, others quite responsibly with community support. Yet, because of the intricacies of the tax powers under which the Harrison Act operated, all were closed, even if unfair harassment was necessary to discourage the operation. It is this past rejection of maintenance clinics in the USA that stops the country from countenancing the idea now – to do so would be to negate almost a century of drug policy. Needless to say, the Swiss experiment was roundly criticized by the guardians of the United States' drug policy.

It is this same refusal even to countenance any change in the status quo that has inhibited the setting up of vital needle exchange programmes throughout the world. That needle exchange programmes reduce the rate of needle-related HIV infection has been documented by just about every respected health authority going including, in the USA, the National Academy of Sciences, American Medical Association, American Public Health Association, National Institutes of Health Consensus Panel, Centers for Disease Control and Prevention, Office of Technology Assessment of the US Congress, American Bar Association, President Bush's and President Clinton's AIDS Advisory Commissions, and others.

The US National Commission on AIDS said this on the subject: *"Legal sanctions on injection equipment do not reduce illicit drug use, but they do increase the sharing of injection equipment and hence the spread of AIDS."* But still the possession, distribution, and sale of syringes remains a criminal offence in much of the USA, and the Federal Government prohibits the use of its funds for needle exchange programmes. The same holds true in much of the world, grappling with a situation where every bone in their body tells them that they cannot do anything that could even be remotely seen to be abetting the illicit consumption of heroin and the reality of a deadly epidemic. This, despite a 1998 World Health Organization report that stated:

"In many countries, drug injecting accounts for more HIV infections than sex. Three-quarters of cases recorded in Malaysia, Vietnam, South-west China, North-east India and Myanmar are among injecting drug users. Although this to an extent reflects the fact that known drug users are tested more systematically than other groups in some of these countries, it highlights drug injecting as a major route of HIV infection. In Western Europe, if one counts infections passed on to the sexual partners and infants of drug users, drug injection accounts for 44 per cent of AIDS cases. In the southern

countries of Latin America, it accounts for nearly a third.

"In Eastern Europe the picture is even more alarming. Some 87 per cent of HIV infections in Belorus are among drug injectors. In the Russian Federation, most infections were spread sexually until 1995, and infection in drug injectors was virtually unheard of. But there has now been a radical shift. In 1996 and 1997, confirmed infections in drug users shot up into the thousands, accounting for four out of every five newly-diagnosed HIV infections."

THE KILLER DRUG

Another of the horrors that campaigners like to present as a deterrent to taking heroin and a reason for its replacement by methadone is, rightly, injury to health. But in this again, reason is clouded by the desire to shock people into acquiescence. One of the greatest weapons in this armoury is the heroin overdose, usually deployed when a spate of deaths in an area are ascribed to a particularly strong batch of heroin. But Stanton Peele, an expert in addiction, has recently called the very notion of heroin overdose into question. He argues that all deaths which are so described are in fact nothing of the sort, but usually due to a cocktail involving among other things, alcohol, barbiturates or the result of ingesting the combination of chemicals often to be found in impure street heroin. Many heroin deaths are, in fact, cases of people drowning on their own vomit (famously Janis Joplin). Heroin may have contributed to the circumstances that produced the fatality, but it is not the sole cause.

To back up his arguments, he points out that when heroin purity levels were much higher, before the Second World War, overdose was almost unknown. His argument is that while these deaths are ascribed to heroin, they fail to alert users to the real dangers, which are to take heroin along with other substances. *"Public officials can generally say any bad thing they want about illegal drugs."* said Peele, *"And they feel no doubt that labelling deaths as overdoses should scare most young people away from drugs. But this message may not have the desired effect and its unintended consequences can be deadly."*

As the Australian National Research Centre made clear: *"Both heroin users and service providers need to be disabused of the myth that heroin overdoses are solely, or even mainly, attributable to fluctuations in heroin."* The myth, though, is a useful one, stressing as it does the inherently dangerous and vicious nature of heroin.

The opium poppy has gone from the Sumerian "joy or rejoicing" to the root of all evil and the cause of innumerable wars and dictatorships. It also enslaves millions with its seductive and transient pleasures. One thing everyone is agreed on is that the "wars on drugs" – there have been many over the last hundred years – have all

THREE STAGES OF PAPAVER SOMNIFERUM - IN BLOOM, THE BUD AND THE BUD AFTER CUTTING.
SOMNIFERUM MEANS BRINGING SLEEP - BUT NOT DEATH

been futile exercises in vote grabbing and attention deflecting. Yet still the politicians carry on with this approach, dealing with heroin as a simple problem with simple solutions. And still they employ heroin as a rallying call for national unity, when there is little else to foster it.

The last US President of the twentieth century, Bill Clinton, whom one might have expected to take a more enlightened approach to drugs, quickly disabused everyone of that idea. Following in the tradition set up by Richard Nixon and followed assiduously by all American presidents since, he too declared war on drugs, which were gnawing away at the very foundations of society. *"We now see in college campuses and neighbourhoods, heroin becoming increasingly the drug of choice,"* he said in 1997, giving no particular evidence for the claim. But the media were happy to jump on the heroin bandwagon, with stories in the press appearing with titles like: *"The Return of a Deadly Drug Called Horse"*, *"Heroin Is Making a Comeback"*, or *"Smack's Back"*. In 1996, *USA Today* declared that *"heroin has its deadly hooks in teens across the nation...the pot of the '90s...as common as beer."* According to Peter Jennings on ABC's *World News Tonight, "the disturbing comeback of heroin among the young is almost impossible to exaggerate... a cautionary tale for all parents and all children."*

On *Turning Point*, Dianne Sawyer claimed *"The statistics are heartbreaking. In the last few years, hundreds and hundreds of young people have died from heroin. Some were among the best and the brightest star athletes, honour students, kids with promise."*

Where all these concerned journalists and broadcasters got their figures from is anybody's guess – presumably from each other. An important point about heroin is that no one really knows the extent of its use – people are hardly going to advertise the fact – and even if you are caught out lying about the extent of the problem you can always claim it was in a good cause.

While some would say that to maintain a constant climate of fear around heroin can only be a good thing, it can also be argued that this only mitigates against any real inroads being made into the treatment of those most affected by heroin – the addicts. Nor can the West expect oppressive regimes throughout the world to develop into compliant and civil liberty respecting governments when, for many of them, the very bedrock of their existence is an illegal trade. Increasingly people – many of them surprising converts – have begun to question the validity of the world's current approach to heroin. On one thing everyone is agreed – the current approach is not working. But no one is quite brave enough to take the first step and suggest an alternative. Such is the power contained in that one word, heroin.

INDEX

BIBLIOGRAPHY

Berridge, V and Edwards, G, *Opium and the People: Opiate Use in Nineteenth-Century England.* Allen Lane, 1981.

Courtwright, D, *Dark Paradise: Opiate Addiction in America before 1940.* Harvard University Press, 1982.

King, R, *The Drug Hang-Up: America's 50-Year Folly.* W W Norton, 1992.

McCoy, A,*The Politics of Heroin: CIA Complicity in the Global Drug Trade.* Lawrence Hill Books, 1991.

Peele, S *The Meaning of Addiction: Compulsive Experience and its Interpretation.* Lexington Books, 1985.

Shapiro, H, *Waiting for the Man: the Story of Drugs and Popular Music.* Helter Skelter Publishing, 1999.